WHAT PEOPLE ARE SAYING ABOUT

THE MASTER COMMUNICATOR'S HANDBOOK

I've seen Teresa and Tim's techniques at work with my leadership team, with transformational results. They've helped us cut through the jargon and communicate with clarity, purpose and vision.
President Donald Kaberuka, President Emeritus, Africa Development Bank

I worked with Tim and Teresa early on in my career with notable results and I've made many a return visit. They scrubbed me of acronyms and schooled me to making everything more relevant and real to my audience. We've now engaged them in training our leaders in a Master Communicators program and I've seen a watershed difference in bringing our work to life.
President Carter Roberts, President and CEO, World Wildlife Fund

Tim and Teresa have mastered the art and science of effective communication. For two years now, I have repeatedly called on their amazing skills to help me prepare for important public statements, presentations or complex sessions with high level counterparts or media. The results are systematically impressive. It works every time!
Hela Cheikhrouhou, Executive Director of the Green Climate Fund

The power of Tim and Teresa's work is that it gave me the confidence to approach public communications without fear – and in fact enjoy it! It has allowed me to convey evidence about development to the general public, including I hope the poor people

whose lives we are trying to improve.
Shantayanan Devarajan, Chief Economist, Middle East and North Africa Region, World Bank

I've watched Teresa and Tim at work for the past 20 years, teaching over 3000 utility professionals from 152 countries how to answer questions effectively and communicate with clarity and authority. I have seen them transform people who were nervous (to say the least) in front of the press into confident professionals. They are the best I have seen and their approach is easy to grasp and effective.
Dr Mark A. Jamison, Director, Public Utility Research Center, University of Florida

I have watched Tim and Teresa coach dozens of young scientists on how to talk to the media and give presentations – their work was truly inspiring. So much so that I participated in their training too! I can honestly say that my confidence in handling the misinformed, false and damaging, and other difficult questions from the media is due to their mentoring. Beyond handling reporters, thanks to their help, I am a better communicator in all my interactions with groups big and small.
Dr Alan Thornhill, Director, Office of Science Quality and Integrity, US Geological Survey; Former Executive Director, Society for Conservation Biology

Teresa and Tim are genuine masters. They have helped me enormously over the years and I am certain that there is no professional speaker working today who would not benefit from reading their book.
Wade Davis, BC Leadership Chair in Cultures and Ecosystems at Risk, University of British Columbia

The Master Communicator's Handbook

The Master Communicator's Handbook

Teresa Erickson and Tim Ward

Winchester, UK
Washington, USA

First published by Changemakers Books, 2015
Changemakers Books is an imprint of John Hunt Publishing Ltd., Laurel House, Station Approach,
Alresford, Hants, SO24 9JH, UK
office1@jhpbooks.net
www.johnhuntpublishing.com
www.changemakers-books.com

For distributor details and how to order please visit the 'Ordering' section on our website.

ISBN: 978 1 78535 153 2
Library of Congress Control Number: 2015939708

A CIP catalogue record for this book is available from the British Library.

Design: Stuart Davies

Printed and bound by CPI Group (UK) Ltd, Croydon, CR0 4YY, UK

CONTENTS

Introduction

Clarity, Leadership, Impact

This book is for people who want to change the world. Here's the challenge: it's impossible to change the world all by yourself. To have an impact, you need to communicate.

In these pages, we will share with you what we have each learned over 30 years as professional communicators – as writers, speakers, broadcasters, reporters, teachers and advisors to leaders of global organizations. We have distilled the essence of this knowledge into useful techniques and models that we teach in our communications courses all around the world. To this we add our insights from our intensive study of neuroscience. In the past two decades neuroscience has revealed much new information about how the brain processes information. Surprisingly little has been written about how to turn the theoretical insights of neuroscience into practical methods of effective communication. We believe we are the first communications professionals to put this together in one book.

You will find our focus on transformation quite different from others'. This is because we have specialized in organizations dedicated to making the world a better place. Our clients include UN and government agencies, multilateral development banks, think-and-do tanks, universities, environmental groups such as WWF, and scientific bodies like the Society of Conservation Biology. These organizations don't exist to make money. They exist to create transformation. Whether taking action on Climate Change, helping to create jobs in poverty-stricken nations, changing policies that discriminate against women or explaining a recent breakthrough in fighting cancer, our clients take on big challenges. To succeed, they know they must communicate powerfully. They also know that credibility is their currency, so they have to be honest, transparent and authentic. For this reason our approach to communications is based on clarity, leadership and impact.

With each person we work with, our goal is to move him or her towards excellence, and in these pages we want to move you towards being the most effective and powerful communicator you can be. Why does this matter? You can have the finances, the human capital, the need and the logistics all in place. But if you fail to communicate why your work is important, you won't get buy-in, you won't get action and you won't create the change you desire.

When it comes to communication, most professionals go wrong by focusing mostly on *output* and not much on *impact*. They think only about what they have to say or write, and very little about how their words will change their audiences' minds. For example, we work with many research report authors who spend a year gathering data and compiling a myriad of facts into a 200-page document. Then they come to us to help prepare for "dissemination." Typically, they allot a half-day for learning how to deliver their message. With a few exceptions, they mostly consider their job done when the report is approved and finalized. Going on a worldwide media tour seems like an after-thought. We wonder how these brilliant people believe their work is going to make any difference if they don't dedicate themselves to promoting it and articulating their ideas on the world stage.

"We like to let the quality of our work speak for itself," they tell us. It's not easy for many experts and authors to accept our response: "Your work does *not* speak for itself. The world will only take notice if you are out there advocating for it."

This book will give you the understanding and the tools you need to become powerful advocates for your cause and your organization. We want you to become a catalyst for transformation. We want you to know that you have the potential to change the world.

Part I

Communicating Ideas

Chapter 1

Spreading Ideas: Memes and Messages

In our 30 years as professional communicators, one of the most fascinating and useful concepts we have come across is the *meme*. A meme is a special kind of idea. It's an idea that spreads. Strictly defined, a meme is a "unit of culture transmitted from mind to mind." Some compare a meme to a "mind virus," which spreads like an infection, the virus replicating itself inside each new host. In the same way, powerful ideas can *replicate and spread.*

The word *meme* was coined by philosopher of science Richard Dawkins. In his 1976 book *The Selfish Gene* he mused about how ideas influence human evolution. Our genes pass on genetic information encoded chemically in our DNA molecules. Through survival of the fittest, the winning genes get passed on to the next generation, driving our physical evolution. Dawkins realized that ideas – memes – function in a similar manner. Our ideas pass on mental information ("units of culture") encoded electrically in our brains' neural networks. Through "survival of the fittest," the winning ideas get passed from mind to mind, driving our cultural evolution. Astonishingly, Dawkins had apparently discovered a second mechanism of human evolution. The difference between genes and memes is that innovative ideas spread much more quickly – at light speed compared to genetic evolution. Our genes could not possibly have evolved fast enough for humanity to make the jump from living in small nomadic bands to dwelling in thriving cities of many millions in just a few thousand years. In short, our *memes* have enabled us to dominate life on the planet.

Think of a meme as like the flame of a candle. Imagine a

ceremony in a great hall in which each person holds an unlit candle. At the front, a match lights a single wick. That first flame gets passed back through the crowd, spreading from candle to candle, so that in just a few minutes, a thousand tiny flames illuminate the entire hall. That's how ideas spread.

What kinds of "unit of culture" are spread this way? It can be something as small and simple as an emoticon -:) – that ubiquitous little sideways smiley face that most of us started tagging on at the end of emails and texts. Or it can be a concept as profound as Climate Change, an idea that causes us to rethink the foundations of our global economy. The range of things that can be considered memes – units of culture that spread – is wide. It includes fashion fads, gossip, new technologies (such as smartphones and solar panels), scientific discoveries, political movements like the "Arab Spring." A song that gets stuck in your head is a meme. The music video of *Gangnam Style* has passed two billion hits on youtube.com as we write this chapter. Imagine if the message you want to communicate could reach such a huge global audience!

What's the difference between a meme and a message? A *message* is a political, commercial, social or moral idea that is being communicated. The root comes from the Latin *missus*, "to send." The emphasis is on the sender. You might be very inarticulate, but as long as you are expressing your idea, it can be considered a message. One might say, "He failed to communicate his message to anyone." With a *meme*, the emphasis is on the *receiver*. If there is no receiver, there *is* no meme.

Replicability is the mark of a meme, and this is crucial when it comes to effective communication. Usually when we communicate we think only about our immediate audience. Do *they* get the message? That's not enough. If your audience gets the message, but not well enough that they can articulate it clearly to others, the idea stops there. If you are seeking to create change – to build an organization, gather support for an issue, develop a new technology or enact any form of meaningful transformation – your ideas must spread from mind to mind to mind.

The evolutionary understanding of memes helps us better understand what really happens on a biological level when we communicate. The West's great thinkers – Plato, Thomas Aquinas, Descartes – all shared a faulty belief that the mind was some ineffable entity that existed in a separate realm that somehow connected to a physical body. We communicated mind to mind with ideas that existed eternally in an "ideal realm."

Instead, envision the mind as being part and parcel of a physical brain, an interrelated system in which the thoughts of the mind correlate with the electrical patterns produced by the cells of that brain. If we see human communication as taking place from brain to brain, the process of communication starts to seem quite difficult. How does the electrical storm in my head jump across space and share a new meme with the electrical storm in your head? While this theoretical question is currently the subject of much interesting neuroscience and psychological research, in practical terms we can derive three insights into what it takes to communicate an idea from one brain to another:

1. Attention

First, get your listener's attention. Now this might sound obvious, yet most of the time when we speak, we are not thinking about whether our listener is really paying attention. Without attention, the neural networks in your listener's brain won't respond to your words. It's like speaking into the phone before the other person has picked up the call. Our first principle is: *No attention, no retention.*

2. Fit-ness

A new meme must fit into the current set of memes in a listener's brain. On a cellular level, an idea is a collection of nerve cells firing in a specific pattern. A new idea creates a new pattern. The new pattern has a better chance of integrating into the person's mind if it meshes well with the existing patterns. It's like clicking a jigsaw puzzle piece into place. The edges of the new piece have to mesh around the edges of existing pieces or it won't fit – and it won't stick. This means if you are going to convey a new idea, you have to know the existing mental landscape of your listener and put your idea in terms that they can most easily assimilate.

The simplest example of this is what happens when someone speaks to you in an unfamiliar language. It's just babble in your ear. But all too often when we try to communicate a new idea to someone, if we don't make it mesh smoothly with what the listener already knows, it's just babble for them, too. We do a lot of work with scientists and economists who often express their ideas using abstractions and mathematical probabilities that most people don't understand. Their audiences don't connect and they fail to communicate. For example, when we work on public communications with utilities regulators, they often like to dive in and discuss rate increases in terms of the need for capital expenditures and investors' rate of return – when they really should start by explaining how this change will affect a customer's electricity bill.

3. Memorability

Our brains are not built to remember; they are built to forget. We screen out most incoming information in order to avoid being overwhelmed. As a result, most of what we process in our conscious minds disappears a moment later. It's as if it goes automatically into a spam folder and gets deleted. Just a tiny percentage of what we experience each day gets integrated into our neural pathways and stored in long-term memory. If you want an idea to spread, you must first make it easy to remember.

Before we explore in detail how to use these insights to make your ideas into good memes, we first want to explain some pitfalls to avoid:

Buzzwords

Sometimes a new meme gets really popular, then just as quickly it becomes passé. In early 2014, the term for a smartphone "selfie" was all the rage. By late 2014, it was already uncool. Almost every organization has its buzzwords. Often these begin as genuinely transformational ideas. But as a word gets overused, it no longer evokes the great concept that lies behind it (see box). It's a kind of linguistic erosion: buzzwords become vague and amorphous terms that cease to evoke a strong mental image. "Every such phrase anaesthetizes a portion of one's brain," as George Orwell famously put it in *Politics and the English Language*.

We think of buzzwords as ideas that are going stale. The trick is to freshen them up again to evoke the original concept in a vivid way. One easy way to do this is by finding the verb or noun at the heart of the buzzword. For example with the tired development buzzword "inclusive growth," one could use the original verb: "growth that includes women and young people."

Overselling

When someone comes on too strong with a new idea, they run the risk of creating resistance in their target audience. It's how we feel when confronted by religious zealots, used-car salespersons and pick-up artists. We suspect an ulterior motive and put up a defensive shield to fend off whatever it is they are "selling." This might seem obvious, and yet we chronically try to shove our favorite ideas down other people's throats. When seeking to spread your ideas, remember to give others the mental space to evaluate and judge for themselves whether or not your new idea will mesh well with their own existing set of memes.

Turning Gold into Straw

A communications officer we know at the World Bank gave us some insight as to how good ideas get degraded. He told us about a typical exchange with his boss. The boss, after reviewing a draft speech written by the communications officer, said: "I want you to add in the word *inclusive* two or three times." *Inclusive* was a hot development buzzword in 2014 – as in, *inclusive growth, inclusive consultations,* and the boss wanted to come across in his speech as being on the leading edge. The communications officer pointed out that the topic of the speech had nothing to do with inclusiveness. "Just put it in!" his boss said firmly. And so our colleague reluctantly threw in the adjective *inclusive* twice and vaguely praised the *inclusivity* of the program the boss was speaking about. So the word ceased to carry any intrinsic meaning and instead became an empty platitude.

Not My Silo

We screen out ideas that don't immediately strike us as relevant. We have to. Most of the time we're working to meet deadlines. We don't have time to think and muse about new ideas unless they are directly relevant. Whole organizations function like this, divided into sealed-off compartments: silos with little day-to-day contact with other parts of the organization. So when you are sharing a new idea, think about it from *their* point of view, then explain how your idea connects to what your audience already cares about. Relevance is critical.

Memes Trump Truth

Just because an idea is true does not mean it will replace a false meme. Once a meme takes root in a person's mind, it is difficult to dig it out. People will defend their memes even as the evidence mounts that they are untrue: a flat earth, the Loch Ness Monster, racial supremacy...the list goes on and on. Similarly, a new meme can quickly spread even if it is false. Urban legends, gossip and political smear campaigns are all examples of how well-crafted lies can quickly morph into common knowledge. Think of that most famous phrase from the O.J. Simpson murder trial: "If the glove don't fit, you must acquit." It forged an unforgettable connection in the jurors' minds between tainted evidence and the verdict. When the glove didn't fit, even though much evidence pointed to O.J., he was acquitted. The lesson for master communicators is to realize that the truth does *not* speak for itself. In a world of memes, the truth needs advocates who can speak for it in a clear and compelling manner.

In summary, *replicability* is the key insight from meme theory for communicators. Thinking about your ideas as memes will help you express them more powerfully and spread them more widely. In the next chapter we will explain practical communications techniques for turning your messages into good memes.

Chapter 2

Crafting Strong Messages

The Four Cs

Let's turn to the practical application of meme theory and how it can help you craft compelling messages that will stick and spread. A powerful message has a meme at the center of it, with supporting language that helps people better internalize the meme and want to pass it on. Great communicators throughout history have intuitively grasped how to do this. In fact, we can illustrate the Four Cs of crafting powerful messages with just one passage from a master orator: Britain's wartime prime minister Winston Churchill.

Here's a paragraph from Churchill's famous speech delivered on 4 June 1940. At this time, many countries had been defeated by Germany, and Britain had suffered major military losses. Indeed, by some accounts, only half the British people expected their country to continue the war. The rest were resigned to defeat. Churchill's speech rallied the nation:

> ...Even though large tracts of Europe and many old and famous States have fallen or may fall into the grip of the Gestapo and all the odious apparatus of Nazi rule, we shall not flag or fail. We shall go on to the end. We shall fight in France, we shall fight on the seas and oceans, we shall fight with growing confidence and growing strength in the air, we shall defend our island, whatever the cost may be. We shall fight on the beaches, we shall fight on the landing grounds, we shall fight in the fields and in the streets, we shall fight in the hills; we shall never surrender...

Even if you are reading these words for the first time, you can doubtless sense the power in them. The speech was turned into placards and posted in homes and offices throughout the nation. Now let's examine how this one paragraph encapsulates our four key characteristics of a good meme:

1. Concise

Get to the core of your message using simple, easy-to-grasp words and short sentences.

Churchill's message of resolve was conveyed perfectly in the short phrases that make up the key sentence of the speech. Delivered aloud, each phrase would sound like a separate sentence:

> We shall fight on the beaches,
> We shall fight on the landing grounds,
> We shall fight in the fields and in the streets,
> We shall fight in the hills;
> We shall never surrender…

Although the speech as a whole has a reading comprehension level suitable for a university student, the core message has a reading level that a 10-year-old could easily understand.

One of our favorite examples of the effect of needlessly long sentences and words comes from the UK's Plain English Campaign:

Before: "High-quality learning environments are a necessary precondition for facilitation and enhancement of the ongoing learning process."
After: "Children need good schools if they are to learn properly."

This is not to say that ideas must be oversimplified. "Everything should be made as simple as possible, but not simpler," as a quote attributed to Albert Einstein puts it. Simplicity eases comprehension, which makes for better memes. There's a neurological basis for why this is so. Our brains don't process written words by reading each letter or spoken syllable individually. We recognize words as whole units of meaning. It's similar to the way Chinese recognize whole written characters. We get the meaning of short, familiar words quickly. Extenuated anomalous verbiage necessitates additional assiduousness. You get the point: longer, less familiar words force our brains to shift gears, slow down and work harder to process the meaning of each combination of letters.

The same holds true with sentences. When we hear or read a sentence, we have to hold all the words in our head until the end in order to make meaning of the sentence. In fact, using MRI imaging, neurologists just recently discovered a distinct and localized region in the brain that lights up when we make sense of a sentence. Short sentences make this easy on our brains. Longer sentences, especially those containing additional clauses (or parenthetical remarks) or insertions of ideas that seem only loosely related – for example if we were to throw in a cooking metaphor about too many ingredients spoiling the stew or something like that – tax the mind, diminish comprehension and make it all too easy for the reader to check out before the sentence winds to its eventual close, a close that becomes downright aggravating should redundancies or secondary ideas be introduced near the end. So don't do that.

Finally, don't try to explain everything in your message. This is especially important for scientists and researchers who relish complexity, comprehensiveness and the interconnectedness of all things. We once worked with a brilliant, grey-bearded economist who was the lead author of a report called *Sustainable Development in a Dynamic World: Transforming Institutions, Growth and Quality of Life*. We were coaching him on how to give good media interviews. He told us, "If I can speak to anyone for 4 hours, I can convince them of the importance of this work. But in under an hour, it's hard to explain anything." The problem of course is that most broadcast interviews are 5 minutes or less, and even most in-depth print interviews last less than an hour. And we're talking about reporters who are *paid* to pay attention because they have to write about it! Most people pay less attention, not more attention, than the media.

2. Concrete

Use strong, concrete words one can visualize. Avoid jargon, technical terms, acronyms and abstract language. In our decades of working with development specialists, we have come to appreciate that within an organization you do need specialist terms and abbreviations to communicate internally. Inevitably, insiders begin to think in this specialized language. Then they start to speak to outsiders as if it is normal, when in fact it is more like a foreign tongue. We tell them that when communicating publically, specialists should view themselves as *translators*. A good communicator has to express concepts in concrete language rather than jargon, so the audience can literally "see" what the specialist is talking about.

We say, "A picture is worth a thousand words." When we speak in concrete language, the image of what we are describing springs to life in the listener's mind; they literally get the picture we are trying to communicate. It also becomes more compelling. We say, "Seeing is believing." Why is this so? Most people are familiar with right-brain/left-brain theory. You doubtless know that the brain's left hemisphere processes words, numbers and abstractions while the right hemisphere processes images, emotions, special relationships and a holistic sense of things. When you speak conceptually, you only stimulate the left brain of your listener. When you speak with visual and sensory details, you stimulate both hemispheres. Also, the images created in the right brain tend to leave an imprint that lasts longer and is more easily recalled than a vague, abstract idea.

Churchill's words paint a clear picture that viscerally evokes the resolve of his besieged fellow citizens: *We shall fight on the beaches, we shall fight on the landing grounds, we shall fight in the fields and in the streets, we shall fight in the hills...* You read this, and you can see it happening. Imagine how flat the speech would have fallen if Churchill had said, "We have to muster our resolve and prepare ourselves for conflict even on our domestic territory." Yet exactly this kind of dull, conceptual language is what we most often get when experts speak.

If you find that you have to use a conceptual word as part of your message, you can back it up with concrete language in an example, story, metaphor or analogy. Here's one example from an Indonesian conservation specialist we worked with. When he first spoke about the importance of his work, he phrased it like this: "Conservation of the Lesan Forest is important due to the many endangered species living there." With a bit of coaching, he revised this to say, "The Lesan Forest is the only home of the rare black orangutan. We must conserve it." The picture of the rare black orangutan sticks.

3. Connected

We have already discussed how a good meme must fit with the existing mental landscape of your audience. But more than that is required to create a great meme. Your listeners must be inspired to *care*. Relevance is crucial to getting an audience to pay attention, remember, and desire to spread an idea. Most communicators are pretty good at explaining why their idea or work matters to *them,* but not so good at explaining why it should matter to others. Our example from Churchill seems like an easy one when it comes to relevance – of course his audience cared. The Nazis were bombing them and there was the very real possibility of Britain being invaded. Even so, historians have written that many people felt this was not their war, but a war of "the high-up people who use long words and have different feelings."[1] By describing fighting taking place in Britain's beaches, fields, streets and hills, Churchill literally brought home to his audience what was at stake for them. It's also important to note how powerfully Churchill uses "We shall" to create the sense of intention shared by all Britons.

To discern how to best connect with your audience, think about these questions:

- Why should the audience care about your message?
- How does it affect your audience's lives?
- Does this message appeal to their interests, especially *higher* values such as: national identity, concern for their children, collective future?
- If your audience is not directly involved, are others affected? Why would your audience care about these others?
- What power does this audience have to affect the outcome? (Are we all in this together?)

To conclude, here are two examples of connecting to your audience delivered by Jim Kim, president of the World Bank, in an NPR interview on Climate Change. Notice the difference between the bland first message and the more powerfully connected second one:

"If carbon emissions are not reduced, average global temperatures will rise between 2 and 5 degrees Celsius by the end of the century."

"If we don't deal with Climate Change now, when my 3-year-old is my age, the coral reefs will all be gone, and the extreme heatwave that killed 50,000 people this summer [in Russia] would happen every year. We can't let that happen to our children and to our planet."[2]

4. Catchy

A meme-like message is made to stick, and our language is filled with lots of tricks that make words memorable. Above, we discussed how good metaphors or arresting visual images do this with our right-brain processing center. We also have sound-processing parts of the brain that respond to alliteration, repetition or rhyme. These turns of phrase add a special kind of *ring* to our language. Have you ever heard a short burst of a once-popular song, a song you hadn't heard in decades, and suddenly you found yourself singing along with the lyrics? You probably don't even know *how* you can remember all the words! Simple literary devices like rhyming and rhythm help us tune in and retain the words. The "ring" makes them resonate. This is evident in the power of Churchill's speech, where he repeats the refrain "We shall fight" over and over again.

Here are a few real-life examples of catchy messages that we helped our clients to craft:

"Africa's growth must be strong, shared and sustainable."
– African Development Bank

"Giving women access to contraceptives saves lives, saves money, saves the planet."
– Population Action International

"Polar bears can only hunt on sea ice. If Climate Change melts the Arctic, they starve. No ice, no bears."
– WWF

And one of our favorite memes, the theme of the TV show *Survivor*:
"Outwit. Outplay. Outlast."

Exercise

Here's a practical methodology you can use whenever you want to turn your message into a meme:

1. Write down your main message.
2. Underline jargon / abstract concepts.
3. Replace those concepts with concrete language.
4. Make it relevant to your target audience.
5. Delete what is not essential.
6. Break it into short sentences.
7. Make it memorable with catchy words and phrases.

In sum, you can use the Four Cs – Concise, Concrete, Connected and Catchy – to make your messages easy to grasp, easy to repeat, and make your listeners *want* to pass your ideas on to others; in short, to turn your messages into powerful memes.

Chapter 3

Structure

The structure of any talk or speech is like a road map. You are the guide, and your listeners are the travelers on the road. To lead them to your destination, you've got to know exactly where you are going and how you are going to get your audience there with you. A bit of strategy is essential. Most people know that a kind of structure is important for presentations, but for a master communicator, a coherent structure is also essential for meeting reports, elevator speeches, individual conversations for a targeted objective, and other forms of strategic communications. Before you start to make notes about what you want to say, answer these three questions:

What's your main idea? Build your talk around a single compelling idea. Your listeners should come away with this idea firmly planted in their minds.
How do you want to change your audience? What is the goal of this talk? Think about how you want to change the audience, even if that audience is one person. Define where they are at the start of your talk (A), and where you want to move them to by the time you finish (B). Your audience's journey is the distance from A to B.

Audience	→	Audience
A. Where they are at the beginning		B. Where they are at the end

This helps you keep our core principle in mind: *Communication is not about output; it's about impact.*

The Building Blocks

Everyone knows there are three classic components to a speech: the introduction, the body and the conclusion. But what most people don't know is the purpose of each of these three parts and how they work together to help the audience make the journey from A to B. To put it succinctly:

- The purpose of the introduction is to get and keep the audience's attention.
- The purpose of the body, or content, is to transmit your information so that it sticks.
- The purpose of the conclusion is to move the audience from information to action.

In sum, a good talk should engage, inform and motivate your audience.

The Introduction

The introduction consists of a greeting, if it's a presentation, a quick outline of the topic, and an attention-getter.

Provide a clear, brief outline. Tell your audience in one sentence the topic of your speech, or, if it's more informal, what you want to talk about. Then briefly go through the elements you're going to cover. Think of this outline as a road map that will help them to follow you. After the outline, tell them directly how your talk will change them. For example, in a speech to your board of directors you might put it like this: "The purpose of my strategy review is to help us take a sober second look at our 5-year business plan, to make sure we are headed in the right direction to meet our long-term goals." This gives them motivation to listen to you.

Get their attention. People are often distracted by the thoughts in their head when a new talk is beginning. Remember: *No attention, no retention*. If your audience is not listening, you might as well stop speaking.

Three effective attention-getters are:

- *Deliver a startling fact,* something unexpected or dramatic that the audience doesn't know, yet that they will immediately realize is important to them. Example: "Most people don't know that still today, nearly half of all child deaths are due to malnutrition."

- *Ask a key question,* a question the audience really wants to know the answer to. Ask this rhetorically – with the implicit promise that you are going to answer the question in the course of your talk.
  Example: "How will your job change in 5 years?"

- *Tell a personal story* that makes them feel strongly connected to you, and establishes your credibility or your connection to the issue (this is for longer, more formal talks).
  Example: "I became passionate about the issue of child trafficking when I met a remarkable woman in Kathmandu, Nepal. She was saving young girls from a life of forced prostitution, and I realized I had to help her, I couldn't turn away."

Here's a great example of an attention-getter used by Kelly McGonigal in her 2013 TED Talk. You can see she is incorporating all three of these approaches into just a few lines:

> I have a confession to make…I am a health psychologist, and my mission is to help people be healthier and happier. But I fear that something I have been teaching for the last ten years

is doing more harm than good, and it has to do with stress…[3]

Content or Body of the Speech

Three main elements must be transmitted in the body of your speech: a clear central idea, the information that makes that idea convincing, and the relevance of your main idea to the audience.

The main idea

Deliver your main point right after your introduction. This is when your audience is listening with their full attention. The mistake many speakers make is to begin with the background, context or history of their subject. They like to lay out all their data and their premises first, and then conclude with their main message. The problem with this is that it requires a lot of attention before getting to the interesting part. It's boring. By the time you get to your important point, no one is listening. Imagine the audience's response to these lines we have heard speakers deliver:

"To truly understand Syria's refugee crisis, let's first look at the history of humanitarianism, beginning with the founding of the Red Cross in 1863. That year at a conference in Geneva the emblem was chosen…"

"So, what is the future of social gaming? Let's begin by looking at some statistics about our company…today we have 10 major games that we run through 13 studios in 6 countries. We are focused on growing our team a lot. We have 1300 full-time employees…"

Our advice: scrap the historical overview that puts your audience to sleep. No one cares. Instead, bring on the main attraction – your main idea.

The challenge here is not just to deliver your idea up on a platter, but to transmit it so that it sticks in the minds of your audience. The chapter on memes provides most of the guidelines for how to do this effectively. Try to make your idea *concise, catchy, concrete, and connected* to what your audience cares about. Here are a few examples of great main messages we have heard from our clients:

"Africa's growth is already strong, but our growth must become shared and sustainable if we want to prosper in the twenty-first century."

"What happens when banks become 'too big to fail'? In the USA, a relatively small elite has become too powerful – powerful in ways that distort the financial sector and damage the rest of the economy."

"Knowledge matters. Having the right information can make the difference between sickness and health, poverty and wealth."

"When it comes to preparing for natural disasters, putting early-warning systems in place is an inexpensive way of saving lives. When a tsunami is coming, a simple alarm bell in a coastal town can give people enough time to get to higher ground."

Supporting information

Support your main message with information that will be convincing to your audience. What does not work are general or vague claims such as: "We all know GMOs are bad for you," or "Trust me, inflation is a major cause of poverty." Also avoid conceptual or technical language or acronyms your listeners might not know. For example: "Our aggregated social welfare indicators indicate an upward trend in GDP may not correlate with a decline in the GINI Coefficient." (You think that was bad?

In our work with development institutions we have heard much worse.)

Clarity is really important at this stage. You want your audience to get each chunk of supporting information in a linear way so they can follow your flow. You can also apply the second C from Chapter 2: be concrete. When you can give your audience a "word picture" of what you are talking about, they form that picture in their heads. This makes them more likely to believe that it is true.

Here are the kinds of information that are most convincing:

- Concrete facts
- Specific examples
- Numbers and statistics – these are crucial to sounding authoritative
- Stories and "eyewitness" accounts
- Analogies and metaphors expressed using visual "word pictures."

Audience relevance

Relevance helps us hold information in our minds. We can't remember everything we hear, but if something has a direct application to our lives and work, we pay more attention and are more likely to store it away for future reference. We are also more likely to care about what is relevant to us, which is important for moving an audience to action. Finally, you want to be sure to speak inside your listeners' frame of reference. For example, use pounds and miles for a US audience, kilos and kilometers in the rest of the world. Here are some key questions to help you find what is relevant to your listeners:

- What's at stake for them?

- What are the risks and opportunities ahead?
- Is there a choice for the audience to make?
- What power do they have to affect the outcome?
- What in your talk connects to their higher values?
- Does your topic connect to issues of morality, justice, identity or the welfare of others?
- What can they do to make a positive difference?

Guideposts: Number your sub-topics

Coming back to our analogy of a road map, it will help your audience know where they are in your talk if you number your main points or sub-topics. Explain this in your introduction, and then during your talk remind your audience where you are: "Now I'll cover my second point, the financing." Use a congruent system: "first…second…third," or "point number one…point number two...point number three." This might sound obvious, but many speakers don't say these markers out loud, or they introduce each new topic with confusing phrases such as "next…also…another thing…an additional point I want to mention." The audience has no idea where such a speaker is heading, nor when the talk will ever come to an end.

Three seems to be a magic number. We can usually remember a list of three things. When it gets to four or beyond, it's easy for a listener to lose track.

When you reach your conclusion, use a final guidepost. Say, "In conclusion…" or "To sum up…" or any other phrase that clearly indicates you have reached the end. This will bring joy to your audience. Listening to even a riveting speaker requires energy and focus; we appreciate the elegance of a speaker who is able to be concise and informative at the same time. Be concise in your final few minutes as you wrap things up.

The Conclusion

Swiftly accomplish the three main tasks of your conclusion:

- Repeat your message
- Move your audience to action
- End with a moment of rapport.

When you say, "In conclusion," this heightens your audience's attention. It's your opportunity to repeat your main message and have them remember it clearly.

Now motivate them to act. You are communicating because you want to accomplish something, reach an objective, change your audience's mind, persuade them to act. So at the end, give your audience something specific to do with your idea and information. It can be something simple, such as inviting questions or prompting a discussion. Or it can be something big: advocating for a new policy, asking for a signature, requesting a vote.

If the purpose of your talk is to interest people in a new program or project and you have a brochure or document with you, you might end by asking whoever in the audience would like a copy to raise their hand. Then give it to them so that they have to reach out and accept it. This simple act creates a physical pattern of taking and accepting the information you have shared. One sometimes hears motivational speakers urging their audiences to make one change in their lives at the end of a talk. It's the same principle: it helps move your listeners from information to action.

For example, one of our clients is a multilateral development agency that wanted to motivate its staff to write blog posts for their new corporate blog. They asked us to give a lecture on social media and step-by-step instructions on how to write a blog post. We ended our talk with an invitation that everyone stay for 30 extra minutes and write a blog post on a work-related topic they cared about. Almost everybody stayed. They wrote 47 posts. Some volunteered to share them aloud, and they blew us away with their quality and creativity. We encouraged everybody to submit their posts to the agency blog. Several of the participants told us they never would have done it if we hadn't asked them to write a post right then and there.

The very end of your talk is an important final moment of rapport. Smile sincerely and make eye contact. Pause without looking away, or sitting down immediately. Stay present with your audience; don't disconnect abruptly.

Tips for Preparation

1. *Speak from notes.* Write down your key points rather than a full text, with one or two sentences per point. Get to the essence of each point. Use large font and leave plenty of white space between points so you don't get lost.

2. *Refine by deleting* extraneous background information, tangents, complaints, or explanations that are too lengthy and convoluted.

3. *Practice out loud.* If this is an important talk or conversation, you should record it and listen to yourself. Are you boring yourself? Do you sound like you're whining? Too many "Ums"?

In conclusion, whenever you are addressing others with a strategic communications goal, think about your audience's journey. How will you move them from A to B? The structure of your talk is like a road map that helps your audience make the journey with you:

- The purpose of the introduction is to get and keep the audience's attention
- The purpose of the content is to transmit your information so that it sticks
- The purpose of the conclusion is to move the audience from information to action.

When you master this simple structure, your audiences will stay with you every step of the way.

Part II

Communicating with Authority

When you speak, you want your audience to see you as an authority, as someone who is confident about their topic. This confidence, when coupled with warmth and authenticity, inspires trust and motivates audiences to act. As humans, we are instinctively tuned to pick out alpha behavior in groups, and we unconsciously pay more attention to those who display this kind of leadership behavior when they communicate. These alpha behaviors are transmitted through our body language, voice and powerful words.

Conveying leadership is especially important when you are not in fact the alpha in the room. What if you are delivering a report to a room full of your bosses? Your behavior *while you are speaking* needs to portray confidence and authority; otherwise your audience may not listen to you at all. You can think of it like this: you may not be the boss, but you *are* the authority over what you have to say.

Chapter 4

Authoritative Body Language

Body language covers everything from our posture and gestures to our facial expressions. As babies, our first language was non-verbal. We stared at and learned to read the facial expressions and gestures of those closest to us before we were able to decipher words and make our own sounds to add to our communication toolkit. We all still have programmed within us that channel that processes non-verbal communication, and that channel is constantly sending impressions about others to our conscious minds. Reinforce your message with these body-language patterns that convey your confidence and authority:

Open Body Language

The most basic lesson in body language is knowing the difference between *closed* and *open* body language. *Closed* body language means you look as if you are physically protecting yourself or concealing something, for example by having your arms crossed over your chest, your hands folded in front or behind you, or hands in your pockets. *Open* body language means you are confident so you feel no need to protect yourself. You stand with your arms at your sides, and sit with your hands apart and on the table.

Studies of both human and mammal groups show that alphas in a group display the most open chest posture. We notice that when speakers get nervous, one of the first things they do is roll their shoulders protectively inwards or upwards towards their ears. As humans, we unconsciously detect this body language and read it as nervous and un-authoritative. Make sure your chest is up and forward, your shoulders down and relaxed, and your arms separate, not glued to your torso but relaxed by your sides and ready to gesture.

The most common question we get from our participants is "But what do I do with my *hands*? They feel so awkward just hanging there by my sides!" It doesn't matter how you *feel*. It's what you look like and what you are conveying to your audience that matters. You are welcome to feel anything you want *after* your talk is done. In the meantime, you have a job to do, and people to influence. Your arms and hands should stay apart and be used to gesture naturally.

Open body language is especially important at the very beginning of your talk. People make up their minds quickly about speakers in the first few minutes. Will this speaker be nervous? Will this speaker be someone I want to listen to? Is this talk going to be boring? Open body language communicates candor, comfort and confidence. Arms crossed or hands folded can communicate aloofness or insecurity.

Gestures

Natural gestures enhance your messages. Even without thinking about it, we use our hands to illustrate the meaning of our words. If we say a "trend is on the rise," it's likely one of our hands will go up as we speak about it. This creates more impact than your words alone. It will be useful to take a video of yourself delivering a talk, so you can see if you are gesturing too much or too little. Interestingly, many of our participants come to us certain that they are using their hands too much when they speak, yet we very rarely see cases of over-gesturing. We *have* had to tell people not to touch their faces or their hair.

Gestures you should avoid: Pointing or jabbing at people, using fists or banging a table to make a point, brushing your hands dismissively at the audience, putting your hands over your mouth, fidgeting with rings, pens or watches.

Your Head

Confidence is literally displayed by keeping a "level head." Hold your head straight when speaking to be at your most authoritative. A tilted head signals receptivity and submissiveness. This is fine when you are having a collaborative conversation and want to convey that you are listening. When you are an alpha delivering information for impact, you want to convey leadership.

Facial Expressions

You want to appear relaxed and natural – your genuine self, and warm, open facial expressions convey your engagement and rapport with an audience. In general, we tell clients to *over*emphasize their facial expressions if they'll be speaking to large audiences or on video. The camera sucks energy from you: you have to put out more energy, and use more expression, to look awake and enthusiastic. Some people have very *few* facial movements when they speak, and that looks robotic and cold. We've also seen some clients who have no idea they frown while speaking, or grimace instead of smile.

This is why it's imperative that you watch a video of yourself speaking. Yes, we know you don't want to. Very few people enjoy this. If it makes you feel better, the video is not exactly what you really look like: it will add pounds and you definitely look much better in person than you do in that little monitor that changes your skin tone and flattens your features. Watching yourself will show you what your face is doing when you speak, and allow you to improve. It's the only way you can become the best public speaker you can be. If what you have to say is important, learn to leave your self-consciousness behind.

Smile

Smiling is one of the most intriguing of human expressions. It's the most important facial expression you can make. Here's why: when we smile – the broader the better – we use specific facial muscles that send endorphins and serotonin – the happy chemicals – to our brains, making us feel positive emotions. Fascinating studies have been done over the years also connecting frequent smiling to longer life expectancies[4] and as a treatment for depression that's equal to the effects of antidepressant pharmaceuticals. How is this relevant to communicating with authority? You want to look relaxed when you speak, and you want your audience to be relaxed and ready to listen to you in a positive frame of mind. Being relaxed in front of an audience shows your confidence. If you think about it, wouldn't you rather listen to a speaker who's relaxed and enthusiastic than one who is stone-faced and you can tell just wants to get it over with? Begin your talk with an honest, broad smile, showing how happy you are to be there. Your audience will smile back at you, creating a positive feedback loop in the room.

Of course if your topic is a serious one, it may not be appropriate to smile during your talk. Smiling where it's not congruent with your words will not make you look authoritative, but as if you are nervous or seeking approval. The same is true with giving fake smiles. As humans we are programmed to spot a fake smile. A real smile involves the muscles around your eyes. Even if your talk has been a serious one, make sure you smile at the audience when you are thanking them at the end. This is your final point of connection, when you transmit your feeling of warmth and appreciation towards your listeners.

Sitting

When we are nervous, we tend to try to take up as little space as possible in a seated position. It's important to sit up straight and take up all the room in the chair, instead of making yourself smaller. This puts energy into your delivery. Slouching lowers your energy. Do not lean to the side, as this can make you look awkward and tilted. Put your arms and hands on the arms of the chair, or if there is a table in front of you, apart and on the table. Avoid crossed arms or hands clasped in front of you like a student. When you are saying something that is particularly important, lean forward for extra impact. The audience will pick up the movement and pay more attention.

Standing

Stand straight with both feet planted on the ground. Do not weave, wander too much, or lean against a table or podium. Some women have a tendency to put one foot behind the other in a "ballerina" pose when they are nervous. This will make you look unsure and unsteady. You should move if the context allows it, but too much movement can be distracting.

After watching countless speakers for many years we have spotted three clear styles to avoid:

The Professor. This style is one we see often in those who have spent a lot of time in academia. This speaker spends most of his or her time speaking either to the floor as they watch their feet, or to the ceiling while pacing slowly about, as if musing aloud to a passive audience waiting to accept the pearls of wisdom.

The Statue. This speaker never moves. At all. They stand frozen in one place for the whole talk. Perhaps their neck moves around to look at the audience, perhaps there are one or two gestures, but otherwise they don't move.

The Mick Jagger. This speaker has graduated from multiple presentation courses and has been told that you need to *move* to generate energy and keep your audience entertained. They cover as much ground as possible, as dramatically as possible; they are a moving target, and it is exhausting just to *watch* them. After sitting through these presentations it is hard to remember anything about the actual content of the speech.

So how much should you move when delivering a talk? It's best to finish a complete thought in one place, and then take a step either to the side or towards the audience to deliver another thought.

Things to watch out for:

- When you move across a stage, notice where audio and power cables are on the floor, so you don't trip.
- Avoid setting up a regular pattern of swaying from side to side – which may hypnotize your audience, and it looks as if you are comforting yourself.
- Don't start your talk so close to the audience that the only movement you can make is backwards.

The Podium

It's best to avoid a podium if possible. Anything that puts a barrier between you and your audience – even a table – is not optimal. If you must use a podium, make sure your gestures are larger than they normally would be, so you are extending your space beyond the boundaries of the podium. For instance, place your hands on the sides of the podium's surface, where the audience can see them. We find that when standing behind a podium, many presenters tend to keep their arms close to their sides, and their hands close together on their notes, with little movement. Remember to be bigger than the podium.

Eye Contact

Eye contact establishes credibility and raises your level of authority with an audience. Avoiding eye contact can make you look nervous or aloof. Research has shown that leaders make more sustained direct eye contact than those in non-leadership positions. During a talk, it's important to make strong eye contact with everyone in the room. If it's a large audience, mentally section the audience into quadrants, and rotate your eye contact among these areas equally. It's best to try and pick out specific people in each quadrant if you can. Speakers are at their best when they are connecting directly to individuals, instead of an amorphous group.

Resist the temptation to only make eye contact with audience members who are smiling at you or nodding enthusiastically. While their positive body language gives you great energy, you may alienate those you never look at. They will feel you are ignoring them. Even if people are not nodding or smiling, you must connect with them. Also keep in mind that the outgoing, smiling audience members may start to feel self-conscious if they feel you are paying too much attention just to them.

Avoid panning or scanning the audience, which means swiveling your eyes around without making real eye contact. This is obvious to those in the room and does not signal confidence. Also avoid looking up at the ceiling when you are speaking. This is a normal pattern when one is thinking and talking at the same time, but it conveys the impression that you are not certain of what you are saying.

A final eye-contact habit to avoid is looking down too much at your notes. If you are reading from your script the whole time, the audience unconsciously thinks that perhaps you don't know your subject that well, or that someone else wrote the script you are delivering. Make sure your notes are in very large font and have lots of white space in between. This way when you look down at the page you can find your place immediately.

This simple technique helps you minimize time spent looking down so you can make lots of eye contact as you speak.

Energy

Let's face it. Most speakers are boring. You don't have to be perfect to be better than most. One of the best things you can do for an audience is pay attention to the energy you are putting into your delivery. Harness any nervous energy you have and use it to push it outwards and speak passionately about your idea. Emotions are contagious and riveting. If you are excited about your topic, display that excitement and your listeners are more likely to be influenced by your words.

Boosting Your Confidence with Body Language

The latest research shows that practicing open body language is not just good for your audience; it's good for you too! Apparently you can derive measurable psychological benefits from keeping your arms open and your chest pushed out. Researchers measured subjects standing in so-called "powerful poses" – a Wonder Woman pose with legs apart and hands on hips, and the Victory Pose, with fists thrust up in the air and chin lifted. They found that after only 2 minutes, levels of the stress hormone cortisol had lowered significantly, and levels of testosterone – the hormone that gives you energy and confidence – had risen. These subjects then performed dramatically better in simulated job interviews than those who had not stood in the power poses before the interviews.

Similarly, when researchers had their subjects sit in "power*less* poses," making themselves as small as possible on chairs with arms crossed and one hand covering their necks, the opposite happened: testosterone levels plummeted, and cortisol levels shot up. These subjects did the worst in the subsequent job interviews.[5] So, by sitting or standing in a protective posture, you are actually making yourself *more* nervous, instead of being comforted.[6]

So, before an important talk or meeting, charge yourself by standing in one of the power poses for 2 minutes. Of course, you don't want to do this where your audience can see you, so find a private place like a nearby washroom where you won't be observed.

Chapter 5

Enhance Your Voice

The best speakers are those who can be heard and can speak with clarity; that's obvious. Learning how to do so if you are not naturally gifted is not so obvious. The good news is there are specific techniques you can follow to get the most out of your voice.

Projection

Learning to project your voice is one of the most important things you can do to improve your delivery. Teresa was a radio broadcaster for 17 years, but when she first began working in radio, her voice was very soft and she was not projecting at all. Her voice coach pointed out that when she spoke, in effect, her words were dropping at her feet, or being blown back inside her chest. He told Teresa to visualize her breath actually pushing her words out towards an audience. The bigger the room, the more energy that pushing would require. That one visualization worked. She was able to project her voice clearly in 1 week.

A large part of voice projection is breathing. Learn to take deep breaths into your diaphragm, not shallow breaths into your chest. Your stomach should expand if you are breathing deeply correctly. Most people speak like this: they breathe into their chests, breathe out, and then talk. At that point, there is not enough air to support the voice to the end of a sentence, or for proper projection. Singers and broadcasters learn to use their voices like this: breathe deeply into the diaphragm, then speak (or sing) *as you are exhaling* – not afterwards. This technique will give you enough air to support your voice without quavering until the end of your sentences.

It's useful to tape yourself delivering your talk, or even just reading a few paragraphs in the newspaper. We all sound different inside our own heads than we sound to everyone else, and it's imperative that you listen to yourself as your audience will hear you. When Teresa first heard herself on tape, she realized she did not fully articulate her words. "To" would come out as "tuh," for instance, and the ends of her sentences often trailed off. Once you know what to change, and practice, it's amazing how quickly you can improve your vocal patterns. Teresa went on to become a senior broadcaster with fan clubs all over the world.

Pause. Pause. Pause.

Just as important, and much quicker to master, is learning to pause. Listeners need extra silences to absorb what you've just said, mentally process the meaning, and then get ready for what you are going to say next. Without those pauses, it's very difficult to recall content. The best speakers know these pauses are crucial to sounding relaxed and in control. Remember that pauses always sound longer to you than they do to the audience.

Resist using filler words like "Soooo..." "you know," "basically" and "like..." Eliminate "ums" and "ahs." These words are verbal clutter that diminish clarity and authority.

We recommend that speakers actually add the word "PAUSE" to their scripts or speaking notes. It's also why we advise lots of white space in your notes. That white space not only makes it easier to find your place in your script; it also reminds you to pause.

Short Sentences

Speaking in short declarative sentences improves clarity and retention. Listeners must hold in their minds all of the words in a sentence as it is being spoken, and only get the full meaning of a sentence at the end. The more words there are, the less will be recalled.

Modulate and Vary Your Speed and Tone of Voice

The ear craves variety. Speak naturally, as if engaged in an interesting conversation. A dull monotone bores people, while unrelenting intensity can tire an audience very quickly. Emphasize important words; in fact, if you are reading from a script, underline the words to emphasize, to remind you during your delivery. Without emphasis, it's difficult for an audience to stay connected and interested. If you speak passionately about your topic, that enthusiasm will be reflected in your voice, and your audience will naturally be excited too.

Voice Patterns to Avoid

High-pitched tones. Shrill, high-pitched voices are extremely difficult to listen to for any length of time. Margaret Thatcher famously learned to lower the pitch of her voice, in order to come across with more gravitas. A high pitch can often be lowered just by relaxing your throat muscles and feeling your voice resonate from deeper within your chest. Your diaphragm, not the back of your throat, should be the source of the energy of your voice.[7]

Voice pitch going up at the end of sentences. Avoid using a rising tone, or uptick, at the ends of your sentences. This turns your statements into tentative questions, and makes you sound less convincing. If every statement sounds like a question? It means you are using your voice the wrong way? Your sentences should end with your pitch going *down*.

Sounding rushed. If you speak too fast, with few pauses, you will come across as nervous, and eager to finish.

A constant loud voice. Some people think projecting your voice means shouting. A constant stream of high energy and high volume is exhausting to listen to after just a few minutes. Vary your tone and add warmth as well as excitement to your vocal energy.

Mumbling. Enunciate your words clearly. Tape yourself to ensure you are speaking with clarity. Your own ears are not the best judge of this; the audio recorder is a neutral party.

Swallowing the ends of your sentences. Some speakers are quite clear at the *beginning* of their sentences, but end in softer tones that cannot be heard. Use shorter sentences to make sure your voice is as strong at the end as it is at the beginning.

Handling Nerves

If you tend to get nervous before you speak, it may affect the quality of your voice. Take slow deep breaths before going on; this will slow down your heart rate. Be aware of any tightness in your throat and jaw. Relax these muscles. It helps to smile broadly for a few minutes before you go on; this will release endorphins and serotonin to your brain. If you have time, practice delivering your speech by over-enunciating the words. This will loosen up your jaw and mouth. Drink something warm, such as herbal tea, instead of cold water. Warm liquids will relax your vocal cords and give your voice more resonance. Do not drink coffee or highly caffeinated beverages; they will dehydrate your mouth.

Chapter 6

Choosing Powerful Words

> The great enemy of clear language is insincerity. When there is a gap between one's real and one's declared aims, one turns as it were instinctively to long words and exhausted idioms, like a cuttlefish spurting out ink.
> – George Orwell, *Politics and the English Language*

As we have stressed earlier, communication is about *impact*, not about output. Yet most speakers we encounter seem to think communication is all about what they say, rather than what the audience will remember. It's as if they think, "I have written my presentation, I will deliver the speech, I have given my interview, and my communication job is now done."

No one will remember every word you say. You have to think about these questions: *What* will they remember? What will you say that will motivate them to act, or to think differently? Are you choosing the right words? Are you delivering them in the best way to make an impact, and influence others? Language is such a powerful tool, and yet most of us don't pay enough attention to strategically choosing the right words for the impact we want to make. Let's look first at language that can immediately detract from the perception of you as an authority.

Language Patterns to Avoid

Self-diminishing qualifiers

Many people are conditioned to prefacing their remarks with statements that weaken what they are going to say next. They do this out of some desire not to seem too assertive with their opinions. But the effect often backfires and makes it easy to discount the value of their words. At worst, it signals to the audience that this person is not worth listening to, so they tune out. For example:

I am not an expert on this, but... Our clients often feel compelled to start this way – even if sometimes they *are* the expert. They feel extreme discomfort eliminating what they see as an important qualifier the audience needs to hear. The issue with these qualifiers is that speakers think the qualifiers attach to the information. However, listeners attach the qualifiers to *you*. What your audience actually hears subliminally is "I'm not really an expert on anything, but anyway, here's what I think on this subject I know very little about..."

In contexts in which you believe you truly need to explain the limits of your expertise, there are ways to qualify your remarks without eroding credibility. Instead of saying, "Now, I'm not an expert on social issues, and haven't read deeply on the social pressures this country is facing...but it seems to me..." you can say, "While my expertise is on macroeconomic issues, I can tell you this about what I see are the societal forces affecting economic performance..." Pointing out where your expertise *does* lie is better than saying you're *not* an expert.

*It's **only** my opinion, but...* This devalues the importance of your opinion.

I'm sure many of you might disagree, but... People are quite ready to disagree with speakers if they have different opinions. You don't have to *invite* them to disagree with you. By saying this, you are putting your audience in a state of disagreement, and they will listen to what you say next through a filter of what is discordant. Also beware of "One could argue that..." Using the word "argue" will likely trigger your listeners' desire to debate your information.

I may be incorrect on this, but... Your audience will be wondering why you are bothering to speak if you may be incorrect. Why waste their time with doubtful information? Everything you say from now on will be received with skepticism.

Tentative language

There's a big difference between directive communication, and communication designed to be tentative. Tentative language is defined as "cautious" or "hedging" language, and it's favored in academic writing where you must be careful of making assertions without qualifiers. Phrases such as *appears to be*, or *perhaps might be attributed to*, or *might be seen in some cases as*, are all examples of tentative, softening terms seen in academic reports. Limiting words, such as *possibly*, *probably* or *likely* also convey uncertainty. This kind of approach does not translate to contexts where you want to come across as clear, assertive and confident. When your goal is to inform and lead, employing a more directive approach with fewer words is more effective.

Tentative: "I don't really have the exact numbers and I may be a bit off, but..."
Directive: "The numbers we have at this point are..."

Tentative: "Without having seen all the data yet, it's hard to say for sure whether this is indeed the best way to go, but I think it may be likely that..."
Directive: "From the data I've seen so far, here's my view on how we should proceed..."

Tentative: "In some developing countries about which we can be reasonably confident of the data, our evidence may point to a

possible supposition that the involvement of a greater percentage of women in the formal sector could have a slightly positive effect on overall GDP rates. So we could perhaps think about addressing gender gap disparities when designing country assistance strategies for those client countries that might possibly be willing to undertake targeted, gender-based labor policies."
Directive: "Our research shows that bringing more women into the labor force can boost GDP rates by nearly 2% a year, and push up incomes by more than 10%. So how can we best assist the countries we work with in investing in women and girls?"

Words and phrases to eliminate

I think. This phrase is often misused, and comes across as tentative, as in: "I think we've found a promising way forward." Speakers use "I think" as a softening term to blunt any possible aggressiveness the listener may construe. The problem is, the statement is weakened, and what is conveyed is uncertainty rather than a weighted opinion coming from an authority. Better to say: "I'm confident this is a promising way forward."
"I think" can easily be replaced by a number of stronger terms, including: "In my view," or "According to my analysis…" You can use "I think" when there *is* uncertainty, or you are still thinking through an idea that is not fully formed, because in such cases you really are describing your thinking process. ("At this point we think this is the best way forward. However, there are other options we need to consider as we get more information.")

Try. "I'm going to *try* to give you a summary of the report..." Don't *try*, as if there is a chance you won't succeed. Do it. Instead say, "Here's a summary of the report…"

Hope. We hear this word all the time from a vast majority of presenters or at meetings:

"*Hopefully,* this presentation will be interesting to you."

"I *hope* I was able to answer all your questions."

It implies that these speakers are not sure they were able to answer questions on the topic they were just presenting! When used in this context, *hope* implies supplication, and puts you subliminally on a lower plane than those you are supplicating to. Instead say:

"I know you'll find this presentation intriguing, and look forward to a lively discussion afterwards."

"Thank you for these great questions. I'm glad we had time for such a rich discussion."

You can use "hope" when you truly mean *hope*. For example, as a noun to mean expectation, vision or desire, as in: "Our hope for you today is that these new tools and techniques will turn you into a compelling and powerful communicator."

Just. This word also devalues and diminishes the worth of what you will say next. Eliminate it.

"I *just* want to add my opinion." "I *just* want to say a few words." "I *just* want to point out something that *I think* is important, and I really *hope* you will too. Let me *try* to be concise..."

Instead say:

"Here's how I see it..."
"Let me add a few words..."
"I want to briefly point out an important aspect of this topic..."

But. This word negates what comes before it. Imagine this: what if your boss called you in and said, "I've been watching you. You're working to full capacity and taking on a lot of new responsibilities, *but*..." Then the phone rings and he or she stops to answer it. What are you thinking? Probably: "I'm getting fired." What if the scenario went like this: "I've been watching you. You're working to full capacity and taking on a lot of new responsibilities, ***and***..." Now the phone rings. This time you're thinking, "I'm getting a raise!"

And can be substituted easily for *but* to make your statements less negative. Instead of: "The government's efforts have been beneficial, *but* there's so much more to do," you can say, "The government's efforts have been beneficial, *and* there's more to do."

Negative language

Speaking in negatives diminishes the power of your messages and can confuse your audience. You are highlighting what is *not* the case or what you do *not* do:

"It's not true to say that I am an argumentative person."

"I can't agree with those who say I am arrogant."

Instead, assert what *is*. This improves the clarity of your speech, and keeps you from sounding defensive. So instead of the negative phrasing in the example above, you could say, "I'm quite agreeable and open to new ideas."

Also, when you state things in the negative, listeners tend to believe the opposite of your denials:

Negative: "I am not a corrupt official who takes bribes. I am not

a crook!"
Better: "I have always been honest. Integrity and honesty are everything to me."

Negative: "We're not here just to grab as much power as we can for our party."
Better: "We are here to work for all the people of Nepal. That is our goal."

Negative: "I'm not saying your comments aren't appreciated."
Better: "I appreciate your comments."

Political strategists often use negative language, because combined with strong visuals and messages that evoke fear they can have a powerful impact on an audience. They work by convincing an audience to move *away* from something, or to *not* choose a particular candidate or legislation. They are rarely motivational or inspirational, and are often bluntly manipulative.

If you strategically decide to use negatives to show your audience what needs to change, always provide a vision of what you *do* want. For example, a development agency's mission statement could be, "We are working towards a world free of poverty." While this phrase explains simply what the organization's efforts are working to move away from, it would be better if said this way: "We are working for a world in which every citizen can thrive and prosper." Statements of leadership are more effective if those you seek to motivate can clearly see the goal they are working towards, instead of the *not*-goal they are trying to avoid.

Confident Expressions

After learning about all the expressions to avoid, here are some ways to begin your statements that increase clarity and impact. They capture an audience's attention immediately and make you sound confident:

I propose...
I urge you to...
I'm confident that...
The facts on this issue are...
My/Our recommendation is...
Let's look at the numbers...
I have 3 points to make. Number 1...
I'll give you 2 reasons why this is so...

Research in psychology and communication has shown that the most memorable words are those that are short and evoke strong emotion. Too often speakers pepper their talks with abstract terms, buzzwords, or bits of conceptual language that wash over an audience and do not make an impact. These are words and terms such as "sustainable development," "inclusive growth," "biodiversity," "value chains," "beneficiaries," "non-food items," and so on. Every industry and professional area has its special language. While audiences may understand these terms, they do not create images in the minds of the listeners, and this is key.

Concrete words are objects or events we can see, hear, feel, taste or smell. So, for example, instead of talking about agriculture, you should talk about coffee growers, or maize crops. Even "crops" alone does not conjure up an image. Be specific. Beneficiaries could be referred to as, "the families in the fishing villages near the dam."

If you need to say one of the buzzwords for a particular audience or context, follow it up with the concrete phrase that will create more impact: "We want to make sure Africa's growth is inclusive growth. That means making sure that women and young people in particular get the opportunities they deserve."

The reason specificity is important is that the brain retains information best when that information is connected to one of our senses. When we speak, our visual sense is the easiest to activate. When you use visual words, you turn on an additional, different part of the human brain from just our left-hemisphere, analytical side. Concrete words stimulate the right side of the brain, which conjures images, triggers memory, and is connected to our emotional and motivational centers. We are rarely motivated or inspired by abstract terms.

For example, "freedom," "equality," are strong words we all can aspire to. However, Martin Luther King Jr added strong visual images to those abstract terms in his "I Have a Dream" speech:

> I have a dream that one day on the red hills of Georgia the sons of former slaves and the sons of former slave owners will be able to sit down together at the table of brotherhood…
>
> I have a dream that one day, down in Alabama, with its vicious racists…one day right there in Alabama, little black boys and black girls will be able to join hands with little white boys and white girls as sisters and brothers.
>
> I have a dream today.

Here's an example, from one of our courses, on how to improve the impact of your statements by using concrete, visual words:

"A World Bank sanitation project aimed at reducing the incidence of cholera in low-income communities was also successful at providing training and jobs for slum-dwellers."

Better: "In the slums of Soweto, or the favelas in Rio, one of the disturbing things you see are open channels of sewage flowing through the streets and alleys...and children playing alongside them. A World Bank community project hired and trained unemployed residents to put in closed PVC pipes into these open channels. Within a few months, the incidence of cholera in these neighborhoods dropped by more than half."

The improved example makes much more of an impact. In fact, we still remember this example word for word though it's been a few years since we first heard it, and we only heard it once.

Whenever possible, use real facts and numbers as opposed to vague, broad statements. Some listeners might hear such statements as just your opinion. For example: "The education budget was quite low again this year, while the military budget was too high."

Better: "This year's education budget was once again less than 2% of total budget allocation. That's the lowest in the region. Meanwhile, the military budget was raised from last year, to nearly 70% of total budget allocation. That's the highest in the region, and actually, one of the highest in the world."

Studies on communication and perception of audiences have shown that people tend to think those who use numbers are smarter speakers. Do not overwhelm the audience, however, with *too many* numbers, and make sure the numbers you use are relevant and key. Comparisons are quite useful to explain the importance of numbers. For example: "A hundred years ago the wild tiger population was over 100,000. Now there are only 3200 tigers living in the wild."

Summary: 7 Elements of Powerful Communication

1. *Show confident body language*
   Stay open. Do not cross your arms. Sit up straight. Relax and occupy your space. Maintain eye contact. Gesture naturally. Smile when you greet your audience and when you thank them at the end.

2. *Speak so your audience listens and absorbs*
   Speak clearly and modulate your voice, so that your words are music to your listeners' ears. Don't rush. Avoid "ums" or "ahs." Emphasize key words by saying them a bit louder than the rest. Pause at the end of sentences, and before or after important phrases to draw attention to each one.

3. *Speak in short sentences*
   Short sentences help your audience process and retain what you say.

4. *Use powerful expressions*
   Choose expressions that show your authority, such as "I propose..." Eliminate those that are weak, tentative, self-diminishing or conceptual. Four words to drop: try, hope, just, but.

5. *Avoid negatives*
   Speaking in the negative can confuse your audience by highlighting what is not the case or what you do not do. Instead, say what is true, or what you actually do.

6. *Be specific*
   Speak about specific facts and numbers; avoid generalities and value judgments. The statement "Ireland did not do

very well last year" can be construed as an opinion. "Ireland's growth rate fell last year from 8% to 1%" is a fact. Be concrete, and use word pictures.

7. *Structure your remarks*
   Keep your audience's journey in mind. How will you move them from A to B?

Part III

Answering Questions

Chapter 7

Answering Questions Effectively

What's the best way to answer a question? Give the answer up front, make your main point clearly, back it up with a good, relevant example, and wrap it up in under a minute. Would you like more information? Now the details…

1. Answer the Question First

Answering questions is one of the most potentially effective forms of communication, because a dramatic tension is created in the act of asking. An exchange is about to take place akin to the electrical impulse passing between nerve cells. There's a power dynamic between one who knows, and one who doesn't, that will shift as soon as the answer comes. And there is anticipation of the unknown, about what is going to be revealed in the answer. All this is the perfect situation for heightened attention, the state in which information can most effectively be transferred from one mind to another.

Sadly many people, especially experts, blow it. They inadvertently shut down this gift of attention. They do this by starting with the background, context or history surrounding the issue before they get around to answering the question. In working with hundreds of economists, environmentalists and scientists all around the world, we've come to the conclusion that this is because experts answer questions in the same format they use for presenting academic papers. They first put forward context and premises, explain methodology, present findings, and at the end, reveal their results and conclusions. But when you do this for answering questions in a media interview, presentation, meeting or simple conversation, listeners easily get confused, frustrated or just plain bored. The tension dissipates without being resolved. People stop listening. As we stress throughout this book, communicating is about *impact,* not about *output*. You may be waxing eloquent about your topic, but if nobody is listening to you, you are just talking to yourself.

Instead, when asked a question, begin *first* with a direct answer to the question. This immediately satisfies your questioners' desire to know the answer. It releases the tension while making them receptive to what you have to say next. As an example, here's the before-and-after response to a question, as answered by a wildlife biologist we worked with recently:

Question: What's the best method of controlling deer populations in North America?
Answer: Well, there are a lot of reasons for deer and human conflict. In some communities, it's deforestation: there's too much building of houses on land that used to be forests. In other communities, there are too many deer because of Climate Change, so the change of vegetation and temperature is causing deer to move into other areas. In other places, it's the lack of predators that has led to overpopulation...

At this point you must be wondering, 'Why is she telling me all this instead of answering my question? Will I need to know this later? Did she not hear my question?' With some coaching, here is the biologist's revised beginning of her answer:

Revised Answer: There are three options: sterilization, regulated hunting and fencing. Each community has to decide which one they are most comfortable with and can best afford. For example...

A direct answer up front gives your listener an organizing

framework for everything else you are going to say. Without that framework, the bits of information just float around untethered in the listener's mind, and they don't know what to do with them. It's like handing a carpenter piles of boards and nails, but no instructions. Better if you say, "We're building a boat. Now, here are the materials, and this is step 1…"

If you get a "yes-or-no" kind of question, go ahead and answer either "Yes" or "No" as the first word, and then elaborate or qualify. These words "yes" and "no" are great signposts that point towards the direction in which you are going to go with your answer.

Some of our participants object that responding to questions using direct answers is a culturally specific mode of communication favored in the USA, Canada, UK and Northern Europe. It is true that some cultures are more naturally direct when it comes to communications. However, in the course of teaching our workshops in over 40 countries, we've discovered that people culturally accustomed to indirect or verbose ways of speaking actually dislike it very much when *other people* don't get to the point. When we worked with Cambodians, Nigerians and Brazilians, for example, they all told us how much they wished their colleagues, bosses and politicians would be more direct when answering questions! This is because answering questions in a professional context is a unique form of communications in which something very specific is requested. It's very different from social communication and conversation, where norms vary widely from culture to culture. What *does* matter when answering questions in a culture that is not your own is tone of voice. There is a difference between *direct* and *abrupt*. If you are from a naturally direct culture, you might have to modulate your voice so it sounds *warmer and friendlier* in order to avoid sounding unintentionally rude. (There are exceptions to starting with direct answers when you are dealing with tricky questions, which we deal with in the next chapter.)

Cultural context does play a role if you are delivering bad news, or if the answer to the question is "no." In cultures that seek to avoid conflict and negative emotion it's best to find culturally appropriate ways to communicate the negative clearly. People within their own culture know how to do this without being crassly direct. Here again, tone and body language convey the real message clearly to the culturally attuned listener. For example, we once heard an American college professor who worked in a Japanese university recall this encounter: He had just finished a faculty meeting in which every other professor had spoken approvingly of a new proposal for the department. On the way out the door, the American said to one of his Japanese colleagues, "Well, I guess we are going forward on this." The Japanese professor looked at him stunned. "Oh, this proposal will never be mentioned again; we were unanimous, it's finished," he replied. "But," said the confused American, "everyone spoke in favor of it!" The Japanese replied, "Ah, but it was the *way* they spoke in favor of it..."

2. Get to Your Main Message Clearly and Concisely

Prepare for any Q&A with a clear idea of the main message you want to deliver – the idea you want to make sure sticks with your audience. After answering the question, immediately link it to your message. This matters most in formal settings such as media interviews, panel discussions or presentation Q&A sessions, where you have a strategic objective to the interaction.

For example, imagine a disability expert answering questions at a conference on transport. She may get questions mostly on costs, but the issue she particularly wants to raise is the topic of how planners perceive disability. She would use the questions as an opportunity to get her message across:

Question: When building mass transit systems in poor countries, should extra money be spent to ensure universal access for people with disabilities?
Answer: Yes. In most cases, it costs very little to design in things like wheelchair ramps and lowered curbs – and much more to add them on at a later date. The point is, disability doesn't reside in the citizen; it resides in the system. If a system is wheelchair friendly, then a person in a wheelchair has no disability.

Without a clear message in mind, such an expert might get caught up discussing complicated details on issues of cost, and never get to the topic she really wants to discuss. This is especially important in media interviews or with potentially confrontational questioners who might ask attacking questions that put you in a corner. Having a clear message enables you to take control and move the exchange in the direction you want it to go.

3. Back Up Your Answer with One Good Example

Experts trip themselves up by trying to be too comprehensive in their answers. Most people don't want to know everything the expert knows. They just want enough to have reasonable confidence that the answer they have been given is true – and they want it to be interesting. In other words, listeners want a good example or some facts and numbers from a reliable source that intuitively makes sense. Providing too much information in an answer is like giving your audience a shopping bag of groceries when they only asked for one piece of fruit. Too much information leaves us numb, not better informed – just as eating a whole bag of groceries would leave us nauseous, not nourished.

Instead of quantity, pay attention to the *quality* of your examples.

Make your example a vivid word picture, something concrete the audience can see in their minds, rather than something conceptual or abstract. Or use exact facts and numbers from reliable sources to boost the credibility of your information. Here's a bad example we heard recently from one of our clients who was investing in a factory in Bangladesh. We asked him questions critical of the project's development impact, because it was costing millions but creating only 50 jobs. At first the investment officer gave an answer like this: "This investment has benefits beyond the factory door. It's part of our effort to revitalize the whole district. It's going to impact the housing sector, manufacturing, education, and increase the viability of new small and medium enterprises. There will even be knock-on effects in agriculture. So we see significant job creation."

He was surprised, annoyed even, when we told him his assertions were not convincing. We discussed what was missing from his answer, and then had him answer the question again: "This investment has benefits beyond the factory door. It's part of our effort to revitalize the whole district. This factory will be the first manufacturer of concrete in the region. Imported concrete is so expensive, no one in the district can afford it. You can't even find it in the marketplace. This has been a real bottleneck until now. We forecast local prices will drop 50%, making concrete more affordable to build homes, schools, new local businesses and markets. The factory is literally providing the missing building blocks for development in this region."

When you hear a convincing example, something clicks in your head. You get it, and that increases your confidence in the speaker. That's why you should aim to provide this kind of information in every answer.

Cultural Preferences

In running our courses globally, we have noticed some interesting preferences when it comes to the kinds of information that convince audiences from different cultures. These generalities don't substitute for knowing your specific listeners; still, they are good overall guidelines:

North Americans in the USA and Canada respond most positively to personal stories and anecdotes (this may be due to the strong individualist streak in US society).

Europeans, especially in the north and west, respond best to numbers and facts, and they usually don't like personal stories in presentations. "Just the facts" fits with their preference for objectivity.

African, Latin, Middle-Eastern and many Asian nations like traditional proverbs and words of wisdom from respected sources of authority.

Scientific, economic and academic audiences share a common preference across cultures for data and numbers from a trusted, referenced source. They also dislike a speaker who seems too certain that his or her research has "proven" anything, preferring information to be described as what current research shows. The disclaimer "more research is needed" seems to follow every analysis, no matter how persuasive.

Universally, we find examples explained with vivid word pictures have broad appeal across all cultures, though some need to see that example in the context of other kinds of culturally convincing information. So, very generally speaking, European audiences would more likely respond to an example paired with data, Africans an example backed by a proverb of common wisdom.

For the most impact, your information should not only be convincing; it should also be significant and meaningful to your listeners. In the example above, if the speaker had left out the detail about concrete prices, we wouldn't grasp how the factory was transformational for the community. Next make sure your example is expressed in terms the audience understands. If you are speaking about finance, use the currency your audience knows best, whether dollars, euros, yen or reminbi. Use comparisons that intuitively make sense to your listeners. For example, when Brazilian environmentalists talk to Americans about the size of the new national park they helped to create in the Amazon, they should describe it as "the size of California and Nevada, combined."

4. End Well

Too many answers end with a whimper, not with a bang. Speakers go on too long, repeat themselves or go off on tangents. The audience tires, stops listening, and you do not come across as a good communicator. Remember, every second your audience is paying attention is work for them. So answer each question in less than a minute and a half. Especially in a Q&A session after a long presentation, the energy of the exchange depends on a lively back-and-forth between you and the questioners. If you go on too long, the energy flags. We see many speakers getting tangled up in their answers, as if they can't figure out how to finish. We have a simple technique that solves that problem. End with a simple one-sentence conclusion that sums up your main message or restates your main point. Prompt yourself when you are ready to end by using words or a phrase that signals to your listeners you are about to finish:

"In conclusion…"
"To sum up…"
"Finally…"

When the audience hears these prompts, it boosts their attention. Your conclusion can now put a cap on your answer and ends it on a high note. For example:

"In conclusion, Europe's economic woes can only be fixed by greater integration. Divided we're weak; together we're strong."

To sum up, whenever you are asked a question, keep your listeners engaged and attentive by following these four simple steps:

1. Start with the answer.
2. Link to your message.
3. Convince with an illuminating and relevant example.
4. Conclude on a high note.

Finally, keep in mind that a question is an opportunity to share what you know with someone who is curious enough to ask. A well-structured answer is one that is clear, organized and enlightening. Such an answer can be an elegant container of knowledge, and extremely satisfying to listeners.

Chapter 8

Dealing with Difficult Questions

Difficult questions can be negative, misleading or even deliberately hostile. The goal for answering these questions effectively is to be clear, authoritative, and avoid sounding defensive. We've analyzed difficult questions and have come up with six of the most common types you're likely to get:

- False charges
- Hostile attacks with some truth in them
- Misleading questions with mistakes embedded in them
- General questions
- Fuzzy, vague questions
- "Pick one!" questions

False Charges

False charges are the most difficult to deal with. These kinds of questions falsely attack either you or your organization with allegations such as, "Your organization is giving bribes to government officials!" Or, "Your program is deeply flawed and will only lead to abject failure in the end. How do you respond?"

Counter false charges by first clearly saying the charge is false, without repeating the allegation word for word. Then directly state the truth. Say what you or your organization did do, instead of denying what your organization did *not* do. This point is absolutely crucial. Repeating negative and emotionally charged words only embeds them further in the minds of the audience. They will come away thinking you are probably guilty and lying about it.

In the example above about giving bribes, if you counter with, "We are *not* giving out bribes!" the audience actually begins to believe there might be some truth to the allegation. Remember Shakespeare's line in *Hamlet,* "The lady doth protest too much, methinks." If you are accused of being a crook and you say, "I am not a crook!" the word "crook" now becomes attached to you. Better to say, "That accusation is false. I am an honest person." That doesn't mean people will immediately believe you, but at least instead of the word "crook" coming out of your mouth, the word "honest" is attached to you.

Here's another example:

Question: "I've heard that some of your project's funds have wound up in the hands of terrorist groups."
Wrong Answer: "I have no idea where you've heard that rumor! I'm really offended by that. Our money is not winding up in the hands of terrorist groups, no way. I mean, do you think we have no clue about what we're doing? I repeat, we are not giving money to terrorist groups!"
Better Answer: "That's completely false. Let me tell you how we monitor the project funds and what the project has accomplished so far..."

Hostile Attacks with Some Truth in Them

Sometimes hostile questions have an element of truth in them, so you can't outright deny the attack. These hostile but true questions can contain highly charged negative words and value judgments that can push you into responding with an emotional, defensive reaction. Negative value judgments are difficult to disprove, so you can end up feeling trapped in a corner.

Here's an example:

Question: "Some of your critics say your organization is very hypocritical. You say you are dedicated to fighting poverty and corruption, but you are working with some very corrupt government officials, right?"

Especially in a conference setting, it's not appropriate to get into a lengthy heated debate about whether or not your organization is "hypocritical." That's a value judgment, not a fact that you can prove or disprove. The key is to get quickly to the legitimate issue embedded within the question, rephrase the question in neutral terms, and turn your attention to matters of fact.

Good Answer: "Look, the issue of corruption is absolutely crucial. The question is, in fighting poverty, is it realistic to ignore the plight of people because we may not approve of the government? Here's how we see it..."

Misleading Questions

Confusing or misleading questions need to be clarified to avoid leaving the wrong impression. If there is a mistake in the question, don't make the questioner feel stupid by saying something like: "Well, it's clear from your question that you don't know this subject very well..." Starting your answer with words such as "Actually..." or phrases like, "You'll be happy to know just the opposite is true..." tactfully cues your audience that you'll be correcting an assumption.

For example, if the question is, "Why are people so worried about Climate Change? A few degrees warmer here and there doesn't sound so bad..." you may feel like replying, "What rock have you been hiding under?"

A more tactful answer would be: "Actually, just a 1 or 2 degree warming can change overall weather patterns, causing more severe floods and droughts and hurricanes. As a result, farmland that once grew corn and wheat could turn into a desert. Here's what the latest research says..."

There are also three kinds of non-hostile questions that can still trip you up. These kinds of questions often catch people off guard and can throw them off balance.

General Questions

General questions are too broad, and you may end up giving a general answer that is boring and so abstract that it leaves people overwhelmed and confused.

For example: "What do you think about the economy?" The audience expects you to focus the question on a specific aspect of this broad topic and provide an interesting and informative answer. You should see these questions as gifts, since you can take them in any direction you wish. The key is to focus and take control.

Good Answer: "The economy has gone through a difficult year, but my recent research on labor statistics shows employment is starting to recover. I can illustrate this turnaround with some recent job figures..."

In two sentences you are talking about your area of expertise, instead of spending 10 minutes blathering on about the economy in general – which no one would be likely to remember.

Fuzzy Questions

These are questions that are so vague you honestly don't have a clue how to answer them. For example: "What about the children?"

The best way to respond is to ask a short, clarifying, question to find out what the real question is, instead of jumping in and floundering around. Open questions lead to more information, while closed questions require a yes or no answer...and then an awkward pause. For example, a closed question would be, "Do you mean the children who have died as a result of the toxins from the factory?" Don't assume or jump to conclusions.

Here's an example of how to deal with a fuzzy question:

Questioner: "What about the children?"
Clarifying Response: "What exactly concerns you about the issue of children?"
Questioner: "Well, you're talking about agricultural projects in developing countries. What about child labor?"
If you still don't know what the questioner is referring to, ask another clarifying question.

Second Clarifying Response: "Specifically, do you have a particular country or project in mind when it comes to child labor?"
Questioner: "Well, actually, I know that in some countries it's unrealistic to expect children won't be working on farms. I'm wondering if any of your projects have found the most effective way to incorporate education in these cases."

One of our clients told us that during his public dissemination of the World Bank's annual *World Development Report* he was asked by a journalist, "What about North Korea?" The problem with fuzzy questions is that, in your effort to answer quickly, you jump to conclusions, and often they are the wrong conclusions. This client said his instinct was to start opining about the political situation in North Korea, but since he'd just taken one of our courses, he applied our technique for answering fuzzy questions. So instead he asked the journalist, "What specifically do you want to know about North Korea?" The journalist replied, "Do you include poverty figures on North Korea in this year's report? I know data has been difficult to find on that issue." Our client said he internally gave a huge sigh of relief. If he'd started talking about the controversial political situation in North Korea the whole press conference could have gone off the rails.

Sometimes you will get vague questions by questioners who really don't know what they want to ask you. You'll quickly figure this out after one or two clarifying open questions. At this point, you want to take your best shot, and ask an insightful question yourself.

Here's an example:

Questioner: "Can you tell me about your projects in Africa?"
Clarifying Response (from an IMF official): "Can you be more specific about the country or region you are most interested in?"
Questioner: "Um. Any country."
Clarifying Response: "OK. We give countries advice and technical assistance on a range of monetary and fiscal policy issues. Any issue in particular?"
Questioner: "Not really, just tell me about your projects in Africa."
Answer: "Ah, certainly. As you know, we don't actually do typical projects in Africa like the World Bank does, but I'm sure you'll be interested to know how we're working with several African countries advising them on banking sector reform. For example..."

"Pick one!" Questions

The last kind of potentially tricky question can throw any speaker into a blank-faced panic. These are questions like:

"So what's the single most important point of this report?"

"That was a great hour-long speech. What's the one thing we should remember?"
"What's the top priority for your organization this year?"

We've seen these "pick one!" questions flummox the most experienced speakers. When we throw this kind of query to our clients, they often respond with confusion: "But it's impossible to say just one! We have five key priorities this year and they are all important. One without the other is meaningless and misleading."

The reality is, you *have* to pick one thing when you are asked these questions. This becomes easier if you qualify it. Here's an example from someone we worked with on IFC's annual *Doing Business Report*:

Question: "What's the main point of this latest *Doing Business Report*?"
Answer: "Since this is an anniversary issue, I'll take a big picture view and say the main point is that all the countries we've been following for 15 years – developed and developing – have made reforms that make it easier for entrepreneurs to start companies and create jobs. Let's drill down and look at impact now…"

This is key: once you answer the question by picking one topic, you are in control and can take the answer anywhere you like. Remember that your questioner often doesn't know exactly what to ask and is saying subliminally, "Look, this topic is very broad. Please just give me one thing to focus on so we can get the discussion rolling." So go ahead and choose something that gives the listener something interesting and relevant.

To Review

- Don't repeat false charges or emotionally volatile words

and phrases. (I am not a crook!)

- Handle hostile questions with a clear denial, then stick to information, don't react with emotion.
- Rephrase hostile but true questions in neutral language, focusing on the legitimate issue embedded in the original question. Don't repeat hyperbolic language and don't get defensive.
- Correct factual mistakes in misinformed questions gracefully and briefly, then get to the point.
- Focus general questions by getting specific quickly and taking your listeners down one road, not a roundabout. Don't answer a broad question with a general answer that gives no interesting, concrete information.
- Focus fuzzy, vague questions by asking open questions in a friendly tone to figure out what the questioner really wants to know. Don't asked closed questions that may lead to awkward tangents.
- When asked to "pick one," do it. Qualify your pick, then take the answer in the direction you want to go. Don't give a laundry list.

Part IV

Creating Connection

Chapter 9

Micro-messages

Communication is so much more than the words we choose or even the body language we use to enhance those words. Charles Darwin was among the first to realize the importance of facial expressions in human communication (*The Expression of Emotions in Man and Animals*, 1872). Researcher and professor Dr Paul Ekman expanded on that research and has spent over 40 years studying communication, emotions and human expressions, including compiling a massive book on every known facial expression and its corresponding meaning (Dr Ekman's life and work was popularized in the US TV show *Lie to Me*). His books and research conclude that humans share some universal facial expressions (even those in isolated, preliterate cultures) that we read instantly, that affect us when we read them, and that we believe more than the words we hear. A raised eyebrow, a smirk, pursed lips, a dramatic eye roll – these are all expressions that evoke strong emotional responses when we receive them. How often have you thought to yourself, "I just don't like John, I'm not sure why. It's a gut feeling; we just don't connect." You may be responding to negative facial expressions "John" is using towards you.

Of course, micro-messages go beyond facial expressions. They include many of the nuanced and often unconscious signals that pass back and forth in almost every interaction. They reveal "what we really feel, and carry powerful clues as to what exists between the lines," according to Stephen Young, author of *Micromessaging: Why Great Leadership Is Beyond Words*.

You might wonder, what's the point of a system of subtle

messages if they are unconscious and most of us miss them? How could that even develop? The answer that makes sense to us is that spoken language is a relatively recent development in humans. It probably happened less than 100,000 years ago. For some five million years prior to that, as our evolution was separating us from the other great apes, we were living in small cooperative bands like chimpanzees or baboons. Researchers who observe these social groups of animals point out a wealth of information communicated without language. Animals like us evolved with tremendous sensitivity to each other's subtle signals. What most likely happened is that as language evolved in humankind, our conscious selves paid attention to the *words* of others, while our unconscious selves stayed tuned to the deeper, older micro-messages.

It was a few years into our partnership before Tim realized that Teresa was skilled at consciously reading micro-messages. We had just finished a meeting with a client about a potential contract with them that year in Denmark. After the meeting, Tim said ebulliently to Teresa, "Well, I guess we are on our way to Copenhagen."

Teresa looked incredulous. "Are you kidding? This is not going to happen."

Tim protested, "But we just spent 2 hours with her telling us what she wants us to do. She just said she was going to bring us over to work with her people. She talked about specific dates!"

Teresa replied, "Didn't you notice that as she was saying that she dropped eye contact completely and looked down, and her voice got lower and quieter?"

Tim was dumbstruck. He had heard only the words. Teresa had read the micro-messages. We never got the assignment.

The Impact of Micro-messages

Positive micro-messages bestow approval, trust and authority on the receiver. Negative micro-messages subtly convey disapproval, lack of trust, and undermine the authority of the receiver. MIT researcher Mary Rowe, PhD, first coined the term "micro-inequities" to define these negative micro-messages and the damage they inflict. The key is to be aware of whether *you* are sending out any of these negative messages and, if you're on the receiving end of them, to make sure they don't affect your performance and demeanor.

Kate, a recent client, is a great example of the importance of being aware of micro-messages you may be sending. Kate is a rising star in her global organization, but she was complaining to us about her communications issue with her manager, Dan. "He hates me! He never speaks directly to me, and sends other people as messengers when he *must* communicate," she said. "And I'm only ever nice to him. For instance, last week he got into the elevator with me and I asked him how his weekend was. He just said 'Fine,' in a brusque tone, then turned away from me and wouldn't even look at me."

Teresa asked Kate, "Close your eyes for a moment. Do you remember the expression on your face when the doors to the elevator opened, and you saw Dan standing there, and then get in the elevator with you?" Kate paused, then nodded. "OK. Can you duplicate that expression now?" Kate opened her eyes and her face changed. Her eyes had narrowed and her lip was curled up a bit. "What are you feeling with that expression?"

"Oh," replied Kate, alarmed. "It's contempt. The truth is, I really don't respect Dan at all and feel he's a waste of space. Yikes, I guess it shows on my face when I talk to him. No wonder he avoids me!"

Here are five types of micro-messages, followed by examples of which ones you can use to enhance your communication and which ones to avoid:

- Facial expressions
- Tone of voice
- Gestures
- Eye contact
- Choice of words

Facial expressions. Examples of facial expressions that send out *positive* micro-messages include smiling; round, open eyes; softened features. Negative facial expressions include frowning, lip biting and exaggerated, fake smiles. Even *no* facial expression is disconcerting. When communicating, we constantly read our listeners' faces to see how they're responding to what we're saying.

Tone of voice. Your voice can either sound sharp and brusque, or warm and soft. Think about how you speak to a child or loved one. It's very different from your tone towards someone you dislike.

Gestures. Research has shown that we feel positive towards those who gesture towards us with their palms facing upward, while downward hand gestures with palms facing the floor connote dismissiveness. Be careful not to point a finger at someone or an audience, unless you are bestowing praise on them. It comes across as hectoring. (A wildlife guide in Rwanda told us that even wild gorillas find it aggressive when humans point at them.)

Open gestures generally convey openness and acceptance. How can we resist liking someone who greets us with arms wide open ready for a big hug? That's preferable to someone who stands with their arms crossed and their body turned away from us as we approach.

Eyes. Eye contact is supremely important for people to feel heard and to feel in rapport.

One woman who worked for a prestigious international organization told us about the time she quit her job, solely because of eye contact. Apparently, her male supervisor would not make eye contact with her. At first she thought it was a cultural issue, as he was from South Asia and she was North American. But she noticed he did make eye contact with the other women in the office...she was the only one he would not make eye contact with. She felt that she could not even discuss this issue; it would sound strange! So she decided to quit. At this point in our training workshop we asked the five others in the room if this kind of thing had ever happened to them; had they ever been compelled to quit a job because of negative micro-messages? They all raised their hands.

One exception is that in many cultures, particularly in East Asia, sustained, direct eye contact may be perceived as intrusive, aggressive or rude. Even in this context, however, eye contact matters. You must still look at an East Asian to show you are giving them your attention, just more generally at their person, just not straight in the eye for a long period.

Choice of words. How often have women complained about being called "girls" in the workplace? In performance reviews, it's been noticed that gender plays a role in the kinds of words used to describe male and female employees. Men are more likely to see words such as "decisive," "results-oriented," "leadership skills." While women tend to see these words crop up: "cheerful," "team player," "easy to get along with."

The words people choose also give you a clue about the power dynamic between you. If you show up for a meeting with someone you see as a peer, and that person starts by saying, "What can I do for you?" they are establishing a relationship in which they have the power and you are a supplicant. Similarly, a person who says, "I'm sorry" when there is no need to apologize is signaling they see themselves in a weak position. For example, starting a scheduled meeting by saying, "I'm sorry to be taking up your time."

Pay attention to word choice to make sure you're not sending unintended micro-messages.

Dealing with Negative Micro-messages

The first viable steps for dealing with received negative micro-messages are:

- Becoming consciously aware of them
- Not taking them personally
- Strategically countering them in ways that create positive change

The Direct Approach

The direct approach can be quite efficient in some instances, and it must be done judiciously. It is easiest with those with whom you have a close rapport. Follow these three steps:

1. State the context and the problem, in specific terms. (Not: "You *never* make eye contact with me," or "You *always* give me an eye roll when I speak.")
2. Give a clear description about the new behavior you are requesting *in the future*.
3. Don't complain; don't justify your request. (Not: "It makes me feel so bad when you do that, and it's just awful!")

Examples:

"Carl, I'm not sure you're aware of this, but the last three times I've come into your office for a meeting, you continued to type and look at your computer, and didn't make eye contact with me. It's hard for me to connect with you if you're multi-tasking. I know how busy you are. Could we agree to keep these meetings brief, and pay full attention to each other?"

Here's one Teresa used recently in a workshop:

"Joan, did you have a question about the last session?"

"No, why?"

"I'm not sure you're aware of it, but you had a frown on your face during the last teaching session, so I thought you might have some questions."

Joan was quite shocked to learn that she had a tendency to frown when she concentrated. We videotaped her during a conversation and she saw it for herself and was appalled. This is an important issue when it comes to micro-messages. We may be sending unintentional messages through our unconscious expressions.

Notes:

- Have this conversation in private.
- Begin by using the person's name. Make eye contact, use a warm voice tone, and keep your expression pleasant and neutral.
- Focus on *future behavior.* Don't complain; don't justify your request.
- Don't make it personal. Just state the facts and the specific behavior you want.
- Do not talk about how the behavior makes you FEEL. Others can dismiss or disagree with feelings and emotions. They can immediately argue, even if silently to themselves, that they are not responsible for the way you *feel.*

Mirroring

Mirroring is the natural tendency we have as humans to copy the body language and facial expressions of others. When people are genuinely engaged, their micro-messages (such as posture and gestures) tend to fall into sync. This facilitates discussion and agreement much like different instruments playing music in harmony. You can use mirroring to your benefit. For example, if your listener has stopped making eye contact and seems distracted, pause for a moment. Hearing you pause, the person will look at you. Now smile a genuinely friendly smile. It will be natural for the person to smile back at you.

However, if you receive *negative* micro-messages, make sure you don't fall into the trap of mirroring those negative signals. If you walk into a room full of people with crossed arms, make sure your body language remains open.

Ally Mirroring

Ally mirroring combines direct requesting and mirroring. With this technique you make a request of a peer or junior for specific behavior to model in the presence of an audience from whom you expect or have already received negative micro-messages.

Example of requesting ally-mirroring:

"Huang, in past meetings with the finance ministry of this country, many of the men had difficulty recognizing the authority of a woman, even though I am the head of the mission team. So here's what I would like you to do: When we enter the room, let me enter first, and I'll introduce myself and the team. If they approach you first, smile and gesture towards me so they will address me first. If one of the officials directs a question to you, please look at me. I will either answer it, or give you the nod to go ahead. I'm confident these steps will avoid any awkward embarrassment so we can focus on the important issues we need to resolve."

One of our client organizations has used ally mirroring among staff members who come from cultures that are not used to speaking up or being interrupted in meetings. During meetings, those who are aware of these issues will step in if someone is interrupting a speaker, or will ask one of their "allies" for their perspective on an issue.

Pattern breaking

If your listener seems stuck in a pattern of negative micro-messages (frowning, distracted, looking bored), change your own body language in a way that will gain his or her attention.

Examples:

- Make a friendly gesture towards him or her
- Take a step towards him or her, in an engaging manner
- Change your position – either stand up or sit down
- Suddenly change your tone of voice (speak more loudly or more softly, or in a warmer tone)
- Ask a question

To sum up, understanding micro-messages is crucial to learning how to create rapport with others in three ways:

1. Becoming conscious of the signals others send provides you with important information about them.
2. Becoming aware of the signals *you* send enhances trust (because your words and non-verbal signals will be better aligned).
3. Identifying and counteracting negative micro-messages of others gives you the ability to respond to them in positive ways and create a more positive dynamic.

Chapter 10

Creating Rapport

Rapport is the "X factor" of great communicators. Mahatma Gandhi, Bill Clinton, Ronald Reagan, Oprah Winfrey, Nelson Mandela, Aung San Suu Kyi – they all create a sense of immediate rapport when they communicate, whether to a huge crowd or one on one. Simply put, rapport is defined as a "relationship of affinity." This means you feel a powerful sense of connection with the speaker. It has been said of Bill Clinton that during his election campaigns he would spend just a few seconds with each person as he worked through a crowd, but in those seconds he made each person feel as if he or she was the most important person in the world to him.

When that sense of connection is established, people enter a unique state. They tune in and open up a more highly conscious receptive channel for communications. This receptivity is actually hardwired into our physiology through the vagus nerve in a way that brain scientists are only just beginning to understand.

The vagus nerve functions like an emotional telephone in each of us that can be connected and disconnected at the flip of a switch. It's a network of nerves that surrounds our digestive system, our heart, throat, jaw and lower face, and is wired into the emotional processing centers of our brain. It connects up our physiology, our facial expressions and our emotions. When we say we have a "gut feeling" or a "heartache," that's the vagus nerve at work, connecting our felt sensations with our emotions.

There is a virtual "switch" in this vagus nerve system, which can immediately put us into one of two modes: "relaxed and receptive" (the parasympathetic nervous system) or highly stressed – the "flight, fight or freeze" state (the sympathetic nervous system, or survival mode). Rapport can only happen between you and your audience when they are in the relaxed and receptive mode.

Think about how hard it is to have a conversation with someone who is angry or fearful or traumatized. We know we need them to calm down before they can hear us or listen to reason.

In the other mode, the parasympathetic nervous system is in charge. It's what kicks in when there are no threats and we feel safe. This "rest and relax" mode is sometimes known as "relate and procreate." In humans, it puts us in a calm state in which we are receptive and open to communication.

To be an effective communicator you need to develop some skill at flipping the emotional switch to the right mode, in other words, to create rapport when it's not happening naturally.

How can we do that? Most people tend to think the ability to create rapport is something extroverts are born with, like the celebrated speakers we listed at the start of the chapter. Or that you can fake it and fool people by being a good actor and reading books about how to win friends and make anyone like you. But in the course of 20 years teaching communications skills, we've discovered that the kind of rapport we're talking about can be learned, and it must be genuine.

Almost everyone knows how to be in rapport with at least one special person in his or her life – typically a family member or old friend. The trick lies in seeing that creating rapport is a natural ability we all have, rather than something that only happens over a long period of time. You can practice creating rapport with people you don't know well, in your workplace or at conferences. The way to do this is by becoming aware of micro-messages, by really seeing the people you're communicating with as individuals you care about, and by consciously sending out your energy to those individuals.

In order to "send out your energy" you first need to generate it inside of you. This takes conscious practice. First, close your eyes and think of the energy you want to project for an upcoming talk or conversation. It could be calmness, it could be excitement, it could be your own definition – like "electric POW!" Feel that energy build inside your chest, starting like a small spark, then building and expanding so it seems to fill you all inside – spreading from your chest, into your stomach, diaphragm, up into your face and into your brain. It sometimes helps to visualize this energy as a color, abstract images, or even a place that inspires you with the energy you're trying to create. For example, you may think of a soft color blue if "calm" is want you want to project, or a recent walk you took along a deserted beach that made you feel calm and grounded. Stay with this energy; remember it. When you open your eyes, be aware of the expression on your face as you feel this energy surging inside of you, filling you. Picture this energy coming out towards the audience with every word you say and in every strong eye connection you make, like a gushing fire hose or an invisible electric current.

Surprisingly, this is actually easier for introverts to master, because introverts already must generate energy within themselves for almost every human interaction. Extroverts turn socialization into energy, so in effect, they bring energy into themselves from others, and then have enough extra to send it out again as well. Receiving energy like this from a speaker is riveting for audiences, and you will achieve great impact. For the speaker, this connection keeps you present and "in the zone." It's absolutely exhilarating.

Micro-messages and Rapport

We covered micro-messages in the previous chapter. Being able to send the right micro-messages is crucial for connection with your audience. Here's a short list of the micro-messages you can use specifically to create rapport (some pertain more directly to one-on-one conversations):

- Friendly eye contact
- Open gestures
- Smiling authentically, with your eyes, not just your mouth
- Warm tone of voice
- Body facing the other person, leaning forward just a bit
- Sending out warm, positive energy through your eyes and voice
- Active listening when the other is speaking, including nodding for agreement
- Showing curiosity and interest by asking open questions
- Early on, asking three questions that elicit a "yes" from the other
- Using words that correspond with the mood or energy you want to set
- Matching your breathing rhythm to theirs

It's hard to imagine consciously remembering all these at once while delivering a speech or having a conversation. Here's a short-cut method that can help you practice and put your own package of rapport skills together all at once:

First, think of someone you know with whom you have great natural rapport. This person could be a parent or sibling, lifelong friend, spouse or mentor. Remember a recent time when you were in conversation with this person and you felt a deep sense of communion and connectedness with them. Picture as clearly as you can the look in their eyes, their face and smile, the tone of voice, their gestures. Notice in your mind's eye all the other subtle signals that formed a part of that conversation and how it made you feel. You will probably want to hold that feeling for a while – because even the memory of being in rapport feels great. When you let it go, write down exactly what micro-messages you remember. If you actually take the step of writing these down, it will help you consolidate all these signals into one package. Then, when you want to create rapport with someone or an audience, you can recall what it was like to be in this state of rapport with this one person, and those subtle signals will all be there for you in this new context.

Mirroring and Rapport

When two people are in deep rapport, they have a tendency to sit or stand in such a way that they seem to be mirrors of each other. As discussed in the previous chapter, this is called *mirroring*. Both may sit with legs crossed, hands folded on a knee, leaning in at the same angle, their heads both tilted slightly to one side. You'll notice this if you watch couples on dates or old friends getting together. Mirroring is a powerful way of expressing rapport. It's as if we not only feel affinity for the other; in a way we also merge identities with the other. At moments like these, people finish each other's sentences or say the exact same thing at the same time.

Synchronization

Besides your body language, you can also mirror the speed, tone and volume of the other person's voice. If the person speaks softly and slowly, for instance, lower your volume and speak at a slower pace than your normal rate. A slow talker will drive a fast talker crazy. Similarly, a quiet, soft-spoken individual will not feel at ease with a loud, boisterous speaker.

Breathing "in sync" is also important. A respiratory specialist told us the fastest way he can help patients in acute respiratory distress is to focus on their breathing, start to breathe with them, and once they are in sync, he can slow down their breath rate.

Active Listening

When you listen attentively to others, you are taking in the information that comes through their words, the information that comes through their voices, and the information conveyed by their rhythm, gestures, postures and facial expressions.

Use open questions and clarifying questions to elicit information; don't *add* your own information. If the other person says they like kayaking, don't immediately interrupt with, "I remember when I went kayaking once, I really enjoyed it…" When you jump in like this, it may seem like you are creating rapport by establishing a common interest. But often what happens is you have refocused the conversation onto yourself, and are no longer in *listening* mode.

Better to say: "Sounds like you really enjoy kayaking."

"Yes."

"Tell me about the most enjoyable kayaking experience you had…"

Yes is a signal of social connection, and social connection feels good to us humans. It feels good to say "yes." It feels like sharing common ground, like belonging to the same group. When we say yes to several questions in a row, another force is exerted. This is the force of pattern. Human beings manage the enormous flow of information through consciousness by organizing information into patterns. Patterns tell us how things fit together; they also tell us what comes next. Sharing a pattern is a powerful form of agreement because it suggests that the agreement will continue through time.

Here's how one skilled practitioner of rapport began a conversation with Teresa recently:

"Oh, you live in Bethesda, Maryland – that's pretty close to Baltimore, right?"

"Yes."

"I lived in Baltimore for a time. I also hear that Georgetown in DC, near where you live, is a great place to walk around, and reminiscent of the rowhouses of Baltimore, is that right?"

"Yes, it is."

"And you must enjoy the cherry blossom season in Washington DC. I've seen pictures and it looks so beautiful!"

"Yes, it's amazing."

You can use all or some of these techniques to bring your listeners into better rapport. Of course, do this subtly, and only when your goal is to create genuine understanding. Salespersons and politicians are infamous for using their skills at faking rapport to achieve their ends. True rapport is authentic, and people can tell. Our aim is to instill in you the awareness that when *you* are truly in rapport with your audience, your impact as a communicator is powerful and magical.

Exercises in Creating Rapport

Two exercises to practice on your own will help you become more aware of elements like energy, mirroring and micro-messages. First, find someone you don't know well, perhaps a new colleague at work, and have a conversation with them in which your only goal is to understand what the world is like for them. Find out what they are working on or what interests them. Take them out for coffee and ask them what they do for fun, or what is their favorite hobby or sport.

During the conversation, use your package of rapport signals and notice the signals they give back to you. Ask open questions to elicit more information. If they are talking about their love of kayaking, ask, "What does it feel like when you're out on the water on a perfect day?" or "How different do you feel after an hour on the water?"

Asking questions that make your audience go into their right brains, to access memory and emotions, is a natural way to create rapport. If you are successful at truly stepping into rapport with this person, you will find by the end of the conversation you will have forgotten all about "doing an exercise," and have gotten completely caught up in the conversation. You will also find both you and the other person have shifted from normal work mode into a state that is relaxed and yet energetic. You will likely both walk away from the conversation with a more positive connection with each other and sense of trust. You will have created rapport.

The second exercise is more challenging: Have the same kind of conversation with someone at work who you find difficult, someone you don't have rapport with – but if you did, your day at the office would be much more pleasant. If you succeed here, you are well on your way to becoming a master at creating rapport.

Establishing Rapport in Public Speaking

The beginning moments of a public presentation are crucial to creating rapport with an audience. If a speaker comes across as relaxed, warm and energized, the audience relaxes and settles in to enjoy the presentation. On the other hand, if the speaker is tense or distracted, the audience will pick this up and find it difficult to concentrate on the content of the talk. Here are a few tactics that can help you come across as your best self and establish good rapport from the very beginning of your talk:

Arrive early. Check the technology if you are using visuals such as PowerPoint. Check the microphone levels. Give yourself time to deal with any last-minute issues so that you are calm and unruffled before your talk begins.

Own the room. Before the audience arrives, stand at the front of the stage where you will be presenting. Imagine the room full of people smiling at you. Walk around with your hands on your hips for at least 2 minutes (a pose that triggers the release of testosterone – a hormone that makes you feel confident, and lowers cortisol, the stress hormone). This helps you take an unfamiliar space and make it into *your* territory.

Cue yourself for success. Develop a ritual that brings out the best in you. It might be remembering an activity you love and are good at – playing the violin, dancing, bowling. Think about what you are like when you are in "the zone" and let those positive feelings fill you as you are waiting to speak. It might be remembering a person who inspires you, or a talented speaker you seek to emulate. The singer Beyoncé has often said that since she is quite shy personally, she has had to create the character "Sasha Fierce" for her performances, and it's really "Sasha" who the audience sees on stage. It may also work to have a soundtrack, or theme song you hear in your head, or actually hear in headphones, that will pump you up. Also, you may simply pick a phrase that energizes you, such as "I got this!" or "It's Showtime!"

Create connection in the first few seconds. After you are introduced, smile warmly and greet the audience. Don't rush. This is the crucial moment of connection, when your audience gets their initial sense of who you are, your level of comfort, authority and confidence. Pause after you say "Good morning," to give them a chance to return the greeting and smile back at you. Your warm demeanor cues the audience on an unconscious physiological level that you are relaxed and comfortable so *they* can relax and be receptive to your words and ideas.

Part V

Changing Minds

Chapter 11

The Visual Channel

Throughout this book, we've emphasized the power of "word pictures" and the value of concrete examples that turn on the visual processing power of the right side of the brain. In this chapter, we'll explore less well-known aspects of how to use the visual channel to persuade and motivate others.

The visual channel in our brain is directly connected to our emotional decision-making centers, specifically to the *amygdala*. The amygdala is an almond-sized cluster of neurons. It's part of the primitive brain that helps us react fast in the face of threats and rewards. If you've ever been scared by a rubber snake or a plastic spider then you have experienced the life-saving power of the amygdala at work. The amygdala triggers our threat response and we jump back; even before we have consciously registered what we are seeing, we are in the air and screaming.

Not all images trigger our amygdala, but when they do, we feel a powerful and immediate urge to act. Think for example of what would happen if you were standing on the side of a busy city street, and suddenly you saw a toddler wandering in traffic. You would probably run forward, grab the child and dodge your way back to safety, literally *without thinking*. This is pretty complicated pre-conscious behavior. You put your own life in jeopardy for a child you don't even know. However, if you had stopped to reflect on your options, the child would be dead. This kind of quick decision-making helped our species survive as we evolved in the forests and savannahs of Africa. The short pathway between visual stimulation and the amygdala means the right-brain ability to understand pictures can be powerfully motivating.

One beautiful example of how actual images can motivate people to act comes from a TED Talk delivered by a friend of ours, Wade Davis. Besides being a best-selling author, Wade is a professor of anthropology at the University of British Columbia and a *National Geographic* Explorer in Residence. For years he has been actively campaigning alongside First Nations tribes to save the province's last great pristine wilderness (known as the Sacred Headwaters) from destructive mining and gas operations. In Wade's TED Talk, he explains factually the threats that would blast mountains and poison rivers, while on screen he shows a cascade of stunning photos of this vast and pristine region of shining mountains and deep green river valleys. The *Geographic*-quality images fill one with awe and move one powerfully to want to preserve this land. As it turned out, the chairman of Shell Canada was in the audience the day of Wade's talk. He met with Wade afterwards, and within a year the company announced they were ending their plans to frack for gas in the Sacred Headwaters.

There are many ways in which visual images – actual or "word pictures" – deeply affect and move us. Especially when it comes to influence and leadership, a master communicator should be aware of them all.

Dominant Images

An image can lodge in our minds as a dominant organizing principle that fundamentally changes the way we think, care and act. For example, recall the long struggle to ban ozone-depleting chemicals in the 1980s. Images from NASA of a "hole" in the ozone layer over Antarctica changed the debate. As a result, every nation signed on to the Montreal Protocol, the world's first globally binding environmental treaty.

Images can be just as powerfully motivating when evoked by words alone. Just one kind of example might be the images used to inspire people to follow their leaders into new and unfamiliar territory: "The Land of Milk and Honey," "Eldorado," and "Greenland" (imagine how Viking settlers must have felt when they landed on that glacier-covered island).

As negative examples, think of the powerful fear evoked by the following images: "The Angel of Death," "The Red Menace," "Nuclear Winter." You can see the powerful grip of such images on the amygdala, urging us to avoid the threat at all costs. In the face of inconclusive evidence that Iraq was building weapons of mass destruction, the Bush administration persuasively made its case with just such a powerful mental image: "We don't want the smoking gun to be a mushroom cloud."

So think carefully about the dominant images you want to evoke to motivate your audiences.

Symbols, Logos and Icons

The Statue of Liberty; the Chinese dragon; the skull and cross-bones; a peace sign; the star and crescent of Islam: visual representations of ideas, institutions or nations carry potent meaning. Wearing the flag pin of your country, a religious symbol around your neck, or in some cases even wearing a particular color can become a bold political statement. Ukraine's Orange Revolution is just one of many examples. Half a million protesters marched in Kiev, wearing orange or waving orange flags as a symbol of opposition to a "stolen" election. In response to this show of unity, the opposition candidate ultimately unseated the fraudulently elected president.

In one organization we worked for, the president refused to step down in the face of nepotism charges. Many people in the organization started wearing a blue ribbon on their lapels, which they said symbolized their commitment to "anti-corruption and good governance." But everyone knew the ribbon was a subversive demand that the president resign. As more and more of the blue ribbons appeared, the pressure mounted until the president quit.

The point is, symbolic objects carry powerful meaning. They stir something tribal in us, something totemic that shapes our sense of purpose and group identity. As a master communicator, think about how you can associate yourself with the right symbols and icons in your communications. Politicians often do this by having icons or symbols in the background. Remember also the negative coverage President Obama received when he was photographed at an official event without an American flag pin on his lapel.

Symbolic Acts

"Actions speak louder than words." Indeed, when people say one thing and do another, we always look to their deeds to reveal their true nature. Mahatma Gandhi understood this well when he defied British rule by walking to the ocean and picking up a handful of salt. The British had decreed salt-making illegal in India. Thousands joined Gandhi in this simple act of defiance, and united the nation in rebellion.

Sometimes a symbolic act may not be deliberate, yet may become a dramatic inflection point. The Arab Spring began in Tunisia with an act of despair and protest. A young fruit vendor, Mohamed Bouazizi, set himself on fire and died in front of a government building after police shut down his fruit and vegetable stand. His self-immolation catalyzed the frustration of millions in the Arab world living under repressive governments. Ultimately it swept away entrenched autocracies in Tunisia, Libya and Egypt.

Especially if you are a leader subject to media scrutiny, with cameras following you around, beware that your every move will be analyzed for potential symbolic acts. Use that fact to send the messages you want through conscious and creative actions. We heard a terrible story from an IMF official who recalled landing in Brazil for meetings and being rushed upon by two ragged children, whom she shunned. Her shooing away of the children was captured on camera and ended up on the front page of a daily newspaper. In fact, it turned out the newspaper photographers had planted the children in order to catch the official in exactly this moment of callous indifference! How different this moment would have been if she had knelt down to talk to the children when they approached her.

So pay attention to how you are being visually portrayed, especially in visits abroad, and find opportunities to create symbolic acts that portray you and your organization in the right light.

The Halo Effect

A person can become a powerful symbol. Aung San Suu Kyi, Martin Luther King, Mother Teresa, Nelson Mandela, the Dalai Lama: they each encapsulate a quality, a value or an aspiration. As a result, anything associated with them tends to take on a similar quality. Any organization's leaders easily fuse in the mind of the staff and the public with the identity of the organization as a whole. This is one reason why leaders must hold themselves to a higher ethical standard.

Beyond leaders, the action of the staff of an organization can also have a positive or negative impact on how an organization is perceived. Recent research has indicated that when organizations take on a collective good work – a charity drive, environmental efficiency programs, community clean-up – it not only boosts how the company is perceived and the morale of those who participated; it even boosts the work performance of those who *did not* take part in the activity.

When you become a visual message

Whenever you appear in public as a representative or spokesperson for your organization, how you look becomes part of your message. Our personal philosophy is that each one of us should wear our clothes and hair in ways that make us feel comfortable and confident. Yet there is no doubt others make judgments about how we look, and those judgments will color how people listen to us. So here are a few strategic rules of thumb that can help your visual appearance enhance your communications. The key is to understand the status dynamic of whatever situation you are entering.

Same tribe. If you want to convey equal status in order to encourage acceptance and open discussion, dress for similarity with your audience. It's easier for people to listen to someone who looks like part of their "tribe" than to an outsider. If you are a public official meeting members of a trade union, wearing an expensive designer suit will hurt, not help, your ability to connect with them. Perhaps rolling up your shirtsleeves would make it easier for them to connect.

Authority. Sometimes you are expected to appear as a leader, respected guest or expert. In these cases, wear clothing your audience will recognize as authoritative or that appropriately supports your high status in this specific context. A friend of ours who runs an underfunded NGO was invited to brief the US State Department about her international work. Her usual attire consisted of casual jeans and worn sandals. We persuaded her to wear business-like attire for the occasion. We told her, "It will help State Department staff hear you better as the authority you truly are." They have since invited her back for regular updates, and she is pleased to be having an influence on an issue she is passionate about.

Respect. Sometimes your appearance should be dictated by the need to show respect to your audience, the venue or the occasion. Typically, this requires more formal wear than normal. If you don't follow protocol – for example not wearing a tie or a polished outfit, you may be perceived as disrespectful. One murky area is wearing the traditional dress of other cultures. Should a Western woman wear a sari to a formal event in India? A kimono to a state dinner in Japan? In such occasions be sure to check with your host to see what will be perceived as respectful.

To sum up, always consider the visual channel as part of your communication. Consciously consider the power of the images, symbols and actions you associate with yourself and your organization.

Chapter 12

Framing

Have you ever had an argument with someone and you have factually proven them wrong, then been astounded that they have not only refused to change their mind, but they seem to be more convinced than ever that their erroneous position is true? If so, then you have encountered the powerful force of framing.

Framing is perhaps the least-well understood concept in communications. Yet when you learn the power of framing, it will fundamentally alter your approach to communications. Framing helps us understand how our ideas are organized in our minds. It helps us grasp how difficult it really is to change someone else's mind. And reframing – the subject of the next chapter – opens up possible ways in which you can actually help someone shift their thinking.

In ordinary usage, "to frame" means to fit something together in order to create a physical structure, such as the frame of a house or a painting. In this chapter we are talking about a "frame of reference" as a mental structure. This mental structure clusters together a set of ideas or assumptions, and shapes how we see some specific aspect of the world.

There are lots of different kinds of these mental frames. Politically, you could speak of a liberal or conservative frame. You could speak of an environmental frame, an economics frame or a social justice frame. We also have frames for all the situations in life that we regularly encounter. We have a "home life" frame and a "work life" frame. An avid whiskey drinker may have a well-developed frame around single malt Scotches, while a music lover might have well-developed frames around various singers and styles she likes. So think of frames very flexibly as like mental boxes in our heads in which similar ideas are all clustered together and connected to each other.

Dr George Lakoff, a psychological researcher at UCLA and author of one of the best books about framing, *Don't Think of an Elephant,* puts it like this:

> One of the fundamental findings of cognitive science is that people think in terms of frames and metaphors...The frames are in the synapses of our brains, physically present in the form of neural circuitry. When the facts don't fit the frames, the frames are kept and the facts ignored.

Why Do We Frame?

Framing is how we make sense of our world. Clustering ideas into frames brings huge evolutionary advantages. Imagine your life if you were always encountering everything for the first time – like how to drive a car. When you rent a car, you don't need to have everything explained to you; you already have a frame in your mind for "car." That frame includes: how to drive, rules of the road, speed limits. Framing makes it easier to do things over and over again.

We also frame our preferences, which helps us make quick, intuitive decisions. For example, when you look at a menu, you have a frame for the sorts of things you like to eat and those you don't. These are going to be different from person to person. Do you sort through the menu with a frame of a healthy diet, a "foodie" gourmet experience, ethical treatment of animals, or to honor religious taboos?

Different Frames Shape Different Realities

When you look at a house you don't see the inner framing; you just see the house. Similarly, we don't see our own mental frames; we just see "reality" as we know it. We don't realize our "reality" has been shaped by our frames. The best proof of framing is the fact that people interpret the world very differently from each other – even though it's the same world. While it may be tempting to believe people who don't think like you are all idiots, it makes more sense to see this variety as a natural result of people with different sets of experience constructing different frames of reference. One simple example is a friend of Tim's who is an expert birder. When they go on hikes together, the friend calls out different bird names as he hears the distinct calls each species makes – he's developed many categories for them. Tim hears only generic "birdsong."

On a grander scale, countries are often ready to go to war over a disputed territory because each side looks at the issue only through their national frames of reference. A good case in point is the currently hot dispute between China and Japan over who owns a few tiny, rocky islands in the sea between them. Each side considers these islands, historically, their territory; because each side has written their own history books, there is no way to find common ground. People who stick to their frames tend to stick to their guns. Our frames can make us rigid if we refuse to see perspectives different from our own.

The Amygdala's Role in Framing

Framing is not just about perception and preferences. It is also about values. Our emotions are wired into our frames. Our frames tell us what we value in our lives, and when that gets threatened, we often react as forcefully as if we were being physically attacked. Have you ever been in an argument and become so angry you started screaming at the other person?

Questions about religion, politics and what we consider right and wrong are so deeply embedded in our frames that when we meet someone with a different set of frames, an argument with them can feel as if we are fighting for our lives.

In such moments our brain literally short-circuits, as the signals of incoming sense data get rerouted to the amygdala. We discussed the role of this primitive part of our brain in the chapter on visual communications. To recap: when faced with a threat, the amygdala quickly activates our primitive emotions: our fight, flight and freeze responses. In today's complex world, our amygdala can lead us to rash acts and poor choices. In zeroing in on a perceived threat, our amygdala-driven brains inadvertently filter out important information. So, for example, we may send a blistering email in reply to someone who offended us – only later realizing that offensive word might have been a typo, not an attack! On a grand scale, a nation might rashly declare war by misinterpreting an innocuous act as an intentional snub or insult – in other words, framing it as a symbolic act.

A recent example of this (fortunately not leading to war) happened when Bill Gates visited South Korea. He kept one hand in his pocket while shaking the hand of President Park. Within the South Korean frame of respect, this informality was perceived as deliberately rude. South Koreans were aghast when they saw the video, and many commentators refused to accept that the "slap" to their leader could possibly have been unintentional. That's the power of the amygdala at work to automatically "frame" our reality for us.

Understanding how framing impacts the amygdala is vital to communications, especially in the face of potential conflicts involving different frames of reference.

Framing in Communications

Fit your facts to your audience's frames

If you speak from your own frame of reference and your audience does not share it, they will not be able to fit your facts into their frames. It will be as if they never heard you – or perhaps interpret what you are saying or doing as something quite different from what you meant.

Tim first became aware of this principle while living in Ladakh in northern India. A German NGO was doing community development work in this remote Himalayan kingdom. One day one of the NGO workers discovered a thin, hard slab of grey material being used by one of the local women as a pan to bake her bread. He was surprised by this, as Ladakhis normally bake their bread on a large hot stone in the oven. The German asked the Ladakhi woman where she got the slab, and she said it was in a pile of unused construction materials left behind from an Indian government building. The slab was much better than a rock, she said, not only because it was so smooth, but also because it didn't get hot when she put it in the oven. Everyone in her village was using them now, the woman enthused. The NGO worker blanched as he realized these were slabs of asbestos.

The NGO got to work on a campaign to explain the medical science of asbestos and the long-term incidence of lung disease it causes. The Ladakhis just laughed. No one was getting sick, they said. Silly foreigners. Scientific facts were just bouncing off the brains of these Himalayan villagers who had no scientific frame of reference. Eventually, the leaders of the NGO asked a senior monk in the area for help. He'd gone to university and immediately grasped the problem. So the monastery issued a decree forbidding the use of these slabs because they contained evil spirits. The community at once threw away the dangerous items.

Interestingly, as Tim recalls the story, some of the German workers were quite irritated at this pronouncement. They didn't like the monastery's inaccurate explanation – although it ultimately proved to be an effective way of describing the dangers of asbestos within a spiritual, Ladakhi frame of reference.

Three-step framing

We have boiled down how to use framing in communications into three simple steps:

1. *Learn your target audience's frames*. Study your audience. Try to see the world through their eyes. What do they value? How do they make sense of the universe? In the example above, if you were trying to persuade Ladakhis not to use asbestos tiles to cook on, you might start by finding out what sort of things fit within the frame of "dangerous, keep away!" for them.

2. *Activate the right frame*. Remember, people have many frames. Think of them as like many pairs of polarized sunglasses a person can wear. You have to use *cueing* (Chapter 14) to direct your audience's attention to the specific frame you want them to pay attention to. This is easier than it sounds in the abstract. If you want to activate someone's frame about swimming, you just start talking about swimming. Use examples, facts, stories and ideas that your audience is familiar with and that fit inside their "swimming" frame. For example, "You remember the last time we went swimming at the beach?" The right neurons will start firing in their brain, activating the frame.

Continuing with the Ladakhi example, you might remind your Himalayan audience of something they already know about things that are dangerous to one's health but that you can't see. It's also important to note that in the story of Ladakh, the fact that the authority who gave the warning was a lama is also significant.

3. *Add your new information/ideas.* Explain how your new information connects with what your listeners already know. Do it with language and metaphors congruent with the audience's frame, as the lama in our story did by invoking the "evil spirits."

Here are two examples of framing in communications:

Example: Scottish Independence Referendum
This was a battle between two separate frames. The Scottish National Party, in power in Scotland, got to compose the question: "Should Scotland be an independent country?" Assuming the people of Scotland have a positive value around independence, framing the question as a "Yes" for them and a "No" for those against independence was a great strategy. It forced the "unionists" to adopt a negative tactic of explaining why Scotland would fail if it tried to become independent. Even though there were plenty of risky economic fears about independence, the "No" side seemed to be losing support as the referendum neared because of the perceived "negativity" of their campaign.

Interestingly, the "No" campaign, led by many English politicians, had adopted the slogan "Better Together." This was an attempt to frame the debate in such a way that highlighted the positives for Scotland of staying inside a "united" kingdom. But by June, just 2 months before the election, the "No" side abandoned this slogan, because it wasn't working. The polls were reporting that people in Scotland found the slogan "meaningless." In other words, while English people thought Scots would value being in a united Britain, this was not really a dominant value for many Scots. The "No" side had failed step 1, and so it had failed step 2, and hence their slogan was not resonating with the people they sought to reach.

The new slogan the "No" side chose was, surprisingly, "No Thanks." Adding that one moderating word resonated with the Scottish people. According to media reports, many Scots were sick of the enmity the campaign had created, souring friendships and family relationships. That tone of declining with polite respect resonated well with them. It gave "No" voters a way to take a stand on the issue that was not absolutist and that did not deny the legitimacy of others to hold a different point of view. While there's no doubt that practical economic considerations played a big part in the decision, this switch to a different framing by the "No" campaign helped stall the momentum of the other side, which may have made a crucial difference in Scotland's ultimate decision to reject independence.

Example: Converting Climate Change Skeptics

A team lead by a Yale psychology professor, Daniel Kahan, conducted an interesting study recently on Climate Change skeptics. They wanted to study the tendency of individuals to select and credit information based on how well it supported their values. In other words they were going to study the effects of framing. The team described the values of typical Climate Change skeptics like this: "Citizens who prize individual self-sufficiency tend to dismiss claims of environmental risk because accepting these claims would license restrictions on free markets…"

The researchers divided their subjects into three groups. First, they asked each group to read a news report. Group #1 read an unrelated news report about a city council meeting on traffic signals (this was the neutral "control" group). Group #2 read a news report about leading scientists calling for regulations on carbon dioxide emissions. Group #3 read a news report about leading scientists calling for more research into geoengineering. (*Geoengineering* refers to large-scale technological schemes to deflect excess sunlight or otherwise artificially cool the planet.) What is important is that none of the three news reports addressed the facts about the reality of Climate Change.

In the next phase of the experiment, researchers asked all three groups to evaluate a different study on *facts* about Climate Change. The interesting result was that subjects in Group #2 – who first read the news report calling for greater regulation of emissions – evaluated the study on the facts of Climate Change as *less reliable* than the group that read the neutral news report about traffic issues. In other words, when *regulation* was proposed as the solution to Climate Change, skeptics were less inclined to believe facts about climate science. Regulation – something that conflicted with their values – seemed to harden their skepticism to the facts.

However, subjects in Group #3 – who read the report on geoengineering – evaluated the study on the facts of Climate Change as *more* reliable. Why? Geoengineering is about managing environmental risks through human ingenuity. So the researchers concluded that as a potential solution to Climate Change, geoengineering "powerfully resonates with persons who have individualistic and hierarchical outlooks." In other words, when the solutions to Climate Change seemed to better fit the skeptic's values, he or she was more likely to evaluate the science itself as valid![8]

The insight gained from this study is not just about Climate

Change skeptics. It's about the power of our frames to influence how we perceive the facts. This is the main message of this chapter: If you want to convince someone, *you must first fit your facts to their frames.*

Chapter 13

Reframing

Arguing with someone whose frame of reference is different from yours can cause more harm than good. When their amygdala kicks in, your opponents are likely to stop reasoning and start defending their positions as if they are being personally attacked. New research (as in the Yale research study in the previous chapter) even suggests that after an argument, people often come away even more committed to their original positions. Why? Because their frames have been reinforced by a strong emotional defense. *Reframing* offers a different way to deal with disagreement caused by conflicting frames. It's the key to helping people change their minds.

Our frames of reference give us only a partial view of reality. As a result there are times when we frame issues in ways that may be widely perceived by others as faulty – even damaging and destructive. It is important to respect other people's different frames of reference, because they are a part of who they are, and these frames are what make up their reality. But sometimes it's also important to know how to reframe beliefs when others' views may be factually wrong or harmful.

For example: someone who believes vaccinating his or her child might cause autism. In reality, there is no clinical evidence for this, while there is a massive amount of evidence that unvaccinated children are at risk of contracting deadly diseases. Or what about someone who believes one race, gender or religion is inferior to another, and that this justifies mistreatment and prejudice? We are also reminded of elected officials who commit to a position, and then refuse to consider new evidence for fear of appearing weak. One such policymaker was quoted in the media saying, "Economists make all kinds of predictions…I don't listen to them." This is a clear indication that such a person is locked into a particular frame of reference and unwilling to hear any new information.

You may choose to help someone reframe:

- if your target audience rejects or ignores important information.
- if your target audience seems locked into a position that is damaging to them (or others).
- if your target audience makes choices that to you seem wrong or stupid.
- if your target audience perceives you or your group in a negative light.

Techniques for Reframing

Here are four steps necessary for reframing:

1. *Create rapport; imagine how the other person sees the world from inside their frames of reference.* Without trust, the other person is not likely to be open to a reframing conversation. The best way to build trust is to be honestly curious about his or her current frame of reference. This kind of conversation has to occur without an agenda to "change them." If you can honestly set that aside and just be interested in why this other person thinks the way they do, then they are more likely to open up. If you listen openly and without the judgment of your own frames, they may surprise you. For example, you might come to better appreciate why they hold the frames they do.

Even if step 1 is all you accomplish, you can shift the perspective of the other person who might hold judgments about "people like you." When we establish rapport with someone very different from us, both parties may end up reframing how they view a whole class of people.

2. *Ask questions to help the other person discover the benefits of reframing (or feel the pain that will occur if there is no change).* Maintaining an attitude of open curiosity, you can ask the other person about potential contradictions in their existing frames. We all have these incongruities between our frames because they were often built haphazardly as we went through life. Each experience or idea we encounter can lead to the construction of a new frame. That new frame may not always dovetail with other frames we've constructed. For example, your parents may have taught you that hard work is the only thing that leads to success, and so you develop a work ethic, and you have that frame inside you. However, in your first job, you may discover that the colleagues in your company who get ahead are not the hardest workers, but those who know how to network and connect with their superiors. So you create that frame about work as well. Either consciously or unconsciously you end up with incongruities and conflicts between your frames. These become a source of internal tension. For example, you might have been raised to honor Thanksgiving dinner with turkey as an important family ritual. Other experiences late in life might have led you to become an ethical vegetarian, and there you are at the feast, stuck with conflicting frames.

So search for these conflicting frames in the other person, and see if you can get the person to open up about them. This is where rapport is important, because merely pointing out logical inconsistencies can be quite provoking and annoying.

As an exercise, imagine you are the advisor to an absolute dictator-for-life in a poor country. You want to help the dictator reframe his attitude towards building a new palace versus providing universal public education for the same cost. As an advisor, let's assume you have already completed step 1, and you understand the dictator well and have his trust. Think first about the kinds of questions you might ask that would nonetheless get you executed on the spot:

"Don't you think you are being selfish putting your own need for glory above your citizens' necessities?"

"Do you want to cause a revolution? What will you say when they put you on trial?"

"Honestly, do you really need a new castle?"

Instead, ask questions exploiting the dictator's conflicting frames:

"In 50 years, what do you think the people of this country will say about you? What kind of a legacy are you going to leave them with?" (One of the dictator's frames is himself as a leader who will be revered for all time; while the conflicting frame is his belief that he deserves the most extravagant show of his power, another is the sense of himself as a benevolent "father" of his people.)

"You tell the people to call you 'father' of the country. What do you think are the best ways you could show your citizens that you care about their wellbeing like a father?"

"If all of your citizens could read and write, what would you like them to write about you in the history books? What facts would you want them to point to?"

"Would you want them all to read about you? Do they have enough education to read well?"

While these questions alone might not be enough to get our hypothetical autocrat to change his evil ways, the point is that the advisor can get him thinking about the tension between his desire for grandeur and his desire to be loved and be remembered well by future generations.

3. *Invite them to imagine a "what if" scenario.* When someone begins to imagine a realistic hypothetical situation, it becomes possible in his or her mind. Our brains tend to hold this rule of thumb: If I can think it, then it could happen. So ask the other person to consider a situation they would consider possible. It could be one of two kinds of situations.

It could be a situation in which they would lose something they value if they keep their present frame. For example, consider a man who doesn't own life insurance because he believes such polices are a waste of money given the slim odds of accidental death. He might shift his frame when asked to imagine exactly what would happen financially to his spouse and children in the event of his sudden death – their home foreclosed, the family thrown out on the street.

The other situation is one in which the person would gain something they value if they dropped their current frame. For example, think of the billionaires who were persuaded by Bill Gates and Warren Buffett to devote large parts of their fortunes to philanthropy. The social value that they gained became quite appealing against a financial loss they would barely feel. To be honest, most people are more easily motivated to change by aversion to loss, rather than attraction to gain. But we think positive motivation works well in the long term, because it can lead to creative and energetic action, rather than a contraction based on fear.

4. *Wait for confusion.* This might sound strange, but one of the strongest indicators that someone has begun the reframing process is that they become confused. Their old mental structure no longer makes sense. Life is no longer secure and predictable. They are in a state of not knowing. It's often an uncomfortable place for people, and so they usually respond by quickly trying to find another frame that makes better sense. As they are reframing, you might find them firing off a string of questions, often fact-based questions. In the examples above, the dictator might start asking about how other great figures of history created their legacies, or the cost of building new schools.

It's a delicate moment in the mind of the one who is reframing. If you are helping someone through this process, now is the time to step back and not talk too much. Answer their questions succinctly, just providing the information they ask for.

5. *Let go of winning.* If it looks as if the other person is in the midst of reframing, and the new frame they are adopting is the one you have been explaining to them, it can be very hard not to feel that you've won a victory. You have to resist this thought with all your might. If you seem triumphant, that can have a negative impact on the other person. They might feel your win equals their loss. You were somehow more powerful than them: your frame was better. All these thoughts and feelings can create resistance to their embracing the new frame.

Here's a real-life example of these five steps in action that took place recently between our friend Mary, a woman in her mid-fifties, and her financial planner, Cheryl. Mary told Cheryl she wanted her retirement savings to be 100% secure. No matter what happened, she wanted a guarantee that her investments would not lose money if the stock market tanked or bonds devalued. Cheryl didn't like this but was unable to convince Mary with charts and graphs. Whenever Cheryl mentioned any degree of risk, Mary would exclaim that risk was what she *didn't* want. So Cheryl listened, and ultimately helped her find some 100% secure government bonds (step 1).

A year later, Mary complained to Cheryl about how poorly her investments had done in a time of skyrocketing stock markets. Cheryl saw that Mary actually had other frames at work than simply avoiding all risk. She used this opportunity to open up the possibility of reframing how Mary could choose to invest differently. Cheryl explained that no risk means no reward. In fact, she said, one thing that was certain was that taking zero risk meant Mary's savings would inevitably lose money due to low interest rates and inflation. Cheryl asked, "Do you want the certainty of losing about 1% of your total value every year?" (step 2).

In the discussion that followed, she asked Mary to consider the "what if" result if Mary kept her current strategy in place in the years after she stopped work and was no longer contributing to her retirement fund. The *certainty of loss*, compounded over 20 years, was a "what if" scenario Mary definitely did not want (step 3).

When faced with this stark choice, Mary was confused. She was surprised to discover for the first time that maybe sometimes some risk was acceptable. Suddenly she had a barrage of questions for Cheryl about different kinds of investments –

questions that up until her reframing began were of no interest to her at all (step 4).

To Cheryl's credit, she thoroughly answered Mary's questions without any attitude, or any hint of "I told you so" (step 5). Mary now enjoys a well-balanced portfolio as she moved from a frame of "no risk equals security" to a frame of "some risk brings rewards."

Four Ways to Reframe

There are doubtless many different ways of reframing, but psychological researchers have defined four distinct categories which are useful to keep in mind if you are helping someone reframe an issue. You can use the acronym ABET, to remember the four ways to *abet* someone in the reframing process:

1. Amplify (or Magnify)
2. Bridge (or Connect)
3. Extend
4. Transform

1. *Frame amplification/magnification* refers to the activation and invigoration of an existing frame of reference so that it overwhelms and replaces the other person's current frame of reference.

Technique: Substitution. This is the easiest technique for reframing. Use it when your audience seems stuck in one frame of reference regarding the issue at hand, but they have another existing frame of reference that could help them better grasp the issue. Your task is to activate this other frame of reference, then help them "turn up the volume" so that this second frame becomes the dominant one in their mind. It's like turning up the music speakers in your home to drown out the annoying music that your neighbors might be playing in their backyard.

Example: Don't Mess with Texas. The government of Texas had a hard time getting its citizens not to litter on the highways. They tried a "Keep Texas Beautiful" campaign that failed abysmally, because of the hyper-individualistic, tough-guy frame that many Texans held about themselves. This gave them the attitude "Nobody tells me what to do!" which was actually triggered by attempts to get them to stop littering! The meme "Don't Mess with Texas" flipped this attitude around, so that littering was about *other people* messing with your homeland. This activated the "Proud to be a Texan" frame which already existed in many Texans, but just wasn't being activated around littering. The government brought the message home with a series of ads showing famous tough Texans like Chuck Norris taking on litterers who dared defile the Lone Star State. One ad showed actor Matthew McConaughey in camouflage gear in a Texas park, armed with a blow gun, shooting a tranquilizer dart into the neck of a littering tourist. The final scene shows a truckload of littering tourists in the back of a pickup truck being dumped across the state line. Littering is thus reframed as disrespectful behavior that only non-Texans would do – and when Texans catch them, well, *nobody* messes with Texas! This frame, now applied to littering, successfully overpowers the old "Nobody tells me what to do!" frame.

2. *Bridging* involves connecting two or more congruent but structurally unconnected frames. For example, a concern about protecting the environment, and a concern about citizens' health and safety.

Technique: Making the Connection. The task here is to reveal to the other person that two of their separate frames in fact overlap. When people realize this, there is often a burst of attention and energy. Why? Because when our frames are better aligned, this creates a sense of integrity. It's like atomic fusion. When two things you are passionate about fuse, it's as if you are able to double your enthusiasm for each. Imagine if your favorite actor were to appear in a movie adaptation of your favorite book. You would really want to see it, right? The principle is the same.

Example: Wildlife Crime. Elephant ivory smuggling in Africa is not just a poaching issue. In the past decade, it has become a lucrative business for organized crime and terrorists, as African warlords kill elephants to finance their armies through sales to Asian crime syndicates. As this atrocity has become widespread across the continent, governments are finding that combatting wildlife crime is also a way of combatting terrorists and organized crime. As a result, the issue has received the attention of global leaders as different as Hillary Clinton and Vladimir Putin who might not have been so committed to a wildlife issue alone.

3. *Frame extension* involves extending the boundaries of an existing frame to incorporate new elements so that the whole frame evolves and expands, like an amoeba engulfing another organism. The challenge with extension is overcoming resistance to incorporating something new. Also one has to deal with skepticism that the revised frame may become diluted, tainted or otherwise weakened by bringing a new element into it. If successful, an extended frame can draw more adherents and create new opportunities, such as political parties that adopt a "Big Tent" approach by reaching out to and including new groups.

Technique: "Absorb and Grow." Those who attempt this kind of reframing must be able to show the benefits of absorbing the new element, or the dire consequences of refusing to change. To make the extension seem as safe as possible, it is helpful to proceed in a way that can be reversed if it doesn't work. You can also demonstrate how similar extensions succeeded in the past.

Example: A decade ago the World Bank extended its frame as a development bank to become a "knowledge bank." The bank's old business was lending money for development projects; as a knowledge bank, the organization reframed itself as a development partner with expertise and experience in what works and what doesn't in international development. This allows it to continue to provide valuable advice even as countries such as China, Turkey and Brazil no longer really need its financing.

4. *Frame transformation* becomes necessary when the existing frames cease to resonate with the person or group's overall perception of reality (that is, their other frames of reference). In other words, when the old framework appears to be crumbling. Revolutions are perhaps the best example of this. The old regime loses control of the people, rebellion succeeds and a new order is established. The challenge here is that as old frames are crumbling, those most invested in the status quo will either cling to it passionately, or else jump recklessly to any new frame of reference (driven more by desperation than reason). The French Revolution comes to mind as a bad example in politics; Quantum Physics, however, serves as a good example of how a new frame can come to dominate a science.

Technique: Plan for the Revolution. The best time to help someone engage in transformational reframing is when major change is unavoidable. If you can help them see clearly what is coming, then they can plan ahead (they will be more capable of reason, less prone to crisis-driven emotion). If you are facilitating transformational reframing, help the others envision "what if" scenarios that are both negative (no change) and positive (with a new frame). It is also important that the new frame being created be congruent with other existing frames, and with the larger belief structures of the audience.

Example: Reframing Africa as the "Third Pole of Global Growth." One of our clients, the African Development Bank, is working hard to reframe the typical Western mindset that Africa is a continent of poverty, crisis and chaos. Africa is also a land rich in natural resources and human potential, and in the twenty-first century it has the possibility of emerging as a powerful economic force. The Western post-colonial "poor Africa" frame is actually part of what is holding Africa back. The truth is, new opportunity alone is often not enough to make people willing to let go of old frames. However, the global economic crisis of 2008 turned into an extended slump that brought several European nations to the brink of collapse. In desperate conditions like this, people from wealthy Western nations are more willing to forego their old frames and look for a new kind of engagement with Africa. Some investors have looked at the remarkable return on investment ratios that are possible on the continent, and are jumping in. Of course, what this example reveals is that transformational reframing often takes a long time, and a lot of hard work.

In summary, framing and reframing are indispensable concepts for master communicators. Only when you understand framing are you capable of helping someone else to let go of stagnant ideas, create a better mental map of the world, and find a path to a more desirable future.

Part VI

Leadership Communications

Chapter 14

Cueing

Cueing is a signal that directs someone, as in an actor taking her cue for an entrance. As a communications tool, the technique of cueing is similar to how yoga teachers or personal trainers work. They use the word "cueing" to mean the verbal and non-verbal ways to communicate to students what move they will perform next, and *how* to do it correctly. For example, "Now you're going to breathe in, hold it, while you relax your neck muscles and lift your torso just a few inches off the mat…" That's what you want to do for anyone you are speaking to. *Cueing is a way of directing and focusing your listeners' attention and telling them how to listen to you.*

So for example, before a presentation, you may want to cue your audience like this: "What I am going to share with you will give you a new perspective on an issue we're all passionate about, a perspective that will open your minds to new, creative ways of doing things." By using the words "new", "open," and "creative," you are cueing their brains to be open to new, creative ideas during your talk.

If you're about to chair a meeting, you want to say something like: "The purpose of this meeting is to be collaborative, and I know you will all want to participate and have something to share." You are cueing your audience that you are making a space for everyone to talk, and that they should think about something to say.

Lady Gaga gave a classic example of cueing an audience on how to feel and listen to her music, during her 2011 "Monster Ball

Tour" as she addressed her fans at Madison Square Garden:

> Tonight, I want you to forget all your insecurities. I want you to reject anyone or anything that's ever made you feel like you don't belong or don't fit in or made you feel like you're not good enough or pretty enough or thin enough or can't sing well enough or dance well enough or write a song well enough or like you'll never win a Grammy or you'll never sell out Madison Square Garden! You just remember that you're a goddamn superstar and you were born this way!

The audience went wild.

Negative cueing is also quite powerful, and it's what most people do unintentionally. They tell their listeners what they want them *not* to think or do. The research on negative cueing is clear: when you tell someone *not* to do something, you are actually cueing them to do the opposite of what you want. Parents already know that saying "Don't break that cup!" to a child will only lead to broken crockery. Much better to say, "*Careful* with that cup."

Here are some examples of negative cueing we've heard from some recent talks:

"I hope I won't be too boring."

"I'm sure many of you will disagree with the points I'm going to make."

"I'm very nervous, I didn't have much time to prepare, so here goes..."

"I don't know how interesting some of you may find what I'm about to talk about, it's a very complicated issue..."

"I'm not as good as the last speaker, and I am positive I won't be able to do as good a job. But I will try if you bear with me..."

In the examples above, the audience is being primed to be bored or to discount the authority of the information coming next. Before a talk, think about the state you want your audience to be in as they listen to you. What mood do you want to create? What emotions are you hoping to elicit? If you want your audience to be excited, use the word in your introduction: "I am so excited to be here," or "This is an exciting day for us," or "I'm excited about the research I'll be sharing with you today."

You particularly want to use cueing at the end of your talks to direct your audience towards what you want them to do with your information. It can be something as simple as: "I'm eager to answer the many questions I'm sure you want to ask." Or as directive as: "Now that you've heard the latest facts on this issue, I urge you to approve this legislation now, when the moment is right."

Here's an example of cueing at the end of a speech recently given by the president of the African Development Bank, Donald Kaberuka, on implementing a gender strategy in all development projects:

> I know everyone in the room agrees with this. We are here not just to reaffirm our attachment to principles. We are here to determine how each of us will implement this new strategy... It can be done. And it is exciting to do. I trust that each of you will play his or her part. I know we all agree: Now is the time for action.

Bill Gates delivered another great example of cueing at the end of his 2007 commencement speech at Harvard:

> You graduates are coming of age in an amazing time. As you leave Harvard, you have technology that members of my class never had. You have awareness of global inequity, which we did not have. And with that awareness, you likely also have an informed conscience that will torment you if you abandon these people whose lives you could change with very little effort. You have more than we had; you must start sooner, and carry on longer.
>
> Knowing what you know, how could you not?
>
> And I hope you will come back here to Harvard 30 years from now and reflect on what you have done with your talent and your energy. I hope you will judge yourselves not on your professional accomplishments alone, but also on how well you have addressed the world's deepest inequities...on how well you treated people a world away who have nothing in common with you but their humanity. Good luck.

Cueing works amazingly well not just in formal communications like presentations and interviews, but also in one-on-one conversations. Most of us go through the day, whether at work or at home, using our words thoughtlessly, and perhaps wondering why we don't have more impact on others. The technique of cueing asks us to put more awareness on the words we choose to use. This awareness can lead to powerful results.

For example, Teresa says her husband has pointed out that she often cues him by saying things such as: "You are the most generous man I know!" He says this only wants to make him *more* generous.

When coaching a client before a big speech at Yale, Tim told him, "Imagine there is someone in the audience whose life is going to be changed when they hear your words. And you're going to speak to that audience as if you are speaking just to that one person. Every word you say is going to irrevocably change their life forever. Make your every word be filled with passion and purpose for that one person." The client told Tim afterwards that it was one of the best talks he ever gave, and that he'd never felt more confident delivering an important speech.

This is the important thing about cueing others: you are cueing them for their own success. You are using the technique of cueing to remind them of resources they possess, and the goals they want to achieve. If a colleague is going to a job interview, instead of saying, "Oh, I hope you get the position!" you could cue them this way: "I know you're prepared for this, and when you are prepared you are at your very best."

Cueing Yourself

Not only can you cue others for success; you can also cue yourself. Self-cueing is powerful, and quite different from self-affirmations.

We first realized the power of self-cueing in a recent media expertise course. During our class we use video cameras to record mock interviews, and before each video session one of the participants, a young woman, would consistently say, "Oh I hate this!" Predictably, her interviews were unsatisfactory.

We pointed out that her exclamations were cueing her for failure, and asked her to think of a positive, realistic statement she could say, which would be a better cue for her success. She thought about it, and then said, "I know this subject so well. I've *got* this." We've worked with this woman for several sessions over 3 years, and this was her best interview.

The next time you're about to do an activity you are unsure or uncomfortable about, think of how you can cue yourself. Instead of "I don't know *how* I'm going to do this!" you can say, "I actually have all the resources I need to get this done." Instead of "Oh, I hate this, I wish I could get out of doing this talk," find your own version of "I've *got* this."

Cueing to Shape the Perceptions of Others

There is one final way to apply cueing. It is especially important for the workplace. How can you cue others so that they perceive you and your work the way that you want them to? In other words, what words would you like people to use to describe you when you are not in the room?

This is something we first heard about from Wall Street CEO Carla Harris, who writes about it in her book, *Expect to Win*.[9] She tells the story of how, early in her career, her boss said to her, "Carla, I don't think you'll last on Wall Street. You're just not tough enough."

Now, as an African American woman who put herself through Harvard Business School, she knew she *was* as tough as anyone, but she realized that wasn't others' perception of her. So she launched a systematic campaign to use the word "tough" to describe herself in casual conversations. When a colleague would ask her opinion about something, she would say, "Are you sure you want my feedback? You know I can be really tough." After 3 months she knew she had succeeded when she overheard two people at work talking in a hallway about her. One was saying, "I'm going to show Carla this presentation and see what she thinks of it." The other said, "Are you sure you want to show it to her? She's so *tough*!"

Carla Harris suggests that you think of three adjectives you want people to use to describe you *when you are not in the room*. These adjectives should be truly congruent with who you are, and also qualities that are valued in your workplace. Use them in conversation to describe yourself whenever possible.

For example, if "strategic" is one of the words you choose, then the next time someone asks you to work on a project you can say, "This is great. I'm a strategic thinker and I can really apply that skill on this project."

If the words you choose are *results-oriented* then you could say, "I'm glad you're asking me to take the lead in this report. I'm all about results, and this report will definitely have an impact."

The mistake many people make is assuming their work speaks for itself. They believe if they *are* strategic, then others will notice. If they are punctual, then others will perceive it. To talk about it seems like some kind of bragging. They don't seem to realize that most people often don't notice much about their co-workers. Even worse, one screw-up often determines the perceptions of others far more powerfully than a dozen assignments done well. The reality is, people are forming their impression of you based on fragmentary information – including gossip and their own inbuilt biases – which might be quite wrong. Of course it is vital that you genuinely possess and use the qualities you tell others you possess!

A client from Asia recently told us she applied this technique with the word "innovative." She was able to measure its success by noting that "innovative" appeared on her performance review a few months after she started using the term to describe herself.

Exercise

Try this now as an exercise for yourself. Write down three adjectives you would like people to use to describe you when you are not in the room:

1.

2.

3.

Now imagine your boss or a colleague asking you a question, and think about how you might answer using one of your adjectives. Obviously you don't have to use all three of your chosen adjectives in every conversation, but repetition is important. When you repeat the same adjectives over and over, after a while people start to associate the quality in relation to you. They can't help it.

You can do this same exercise for your ideas or your goals at work. If you are part of a team with common objectives, make sure everyone uses the same adjectives to best spread the perception you want. Here are some examples:

Adjective: *game-changer*. Used in a conversation: "This project is a *game-changer*. It's going to give millions of people too poor to have a bank account a way to save for their children's futures."

Adjective: *affordable*. Used in a conversation: "The best thing about this program is that it's *affordable*. In fact, within 2 years it will save several millions over the old way of doing things."

Now that you know how to effectively use cueing, you'll want to use this powerful tool every time you communicate strategically.

Chapter 15

Vision

Vision is the single most important element for creating transformation through communication. Vision draws an organization, a community or a nation forward together, and it does so in a very specific way. Here's how we define it:

A vision is a picture of an imagined future, a future people desire for themselves, and a future that will take collective effort to create.

When these three elements combine, you have the ingredients for *storytelling* about how we will get from an unsatisfactory present to a desired future that with effort we can attain. This is the essence of vision: it's how we write the next chapter of our collective destiny.

The key to a powerful vision is simply this: People who hear your story of the future want to make it *their* story of the future too. The world's great visionaries express the dreams and aspirations of *their* people. You can see these principles brought to light in the words of four great visionaries of the twentieth century:

Martin Luther King Jr: "I have a dream that one day little black boys and girls will be holding hands with little white boys and girls…"

Mahatma Gandhi: "A small body of determined spirits fired by an unquenchable faith in their mission can alter the course of history."

Nelson Mandela: "We fight for and visualize a future in which all shall, without regard to race, color, creed or sex, have the right to vote and be voted into all elective organs of state."

Aung San Suu Kyi: "I don't believe in people just hoping. We work for what we want. I always say that one has no right to hope without endeavor...we are confident that we will get to the negotiation table..."

These three elements – a *future picture that people desire, requiring effort* – must be conveyed as the story of the audience's journey to make the vision a reality. When people see the story unfolding in their mind, they begin to grasp that it is possible: racial equality for all Americans; votes for every citizen in South Africa; independence from Britain and self-determination for Indians; democracy in Myanmar. If it can be imagined, it can happen. This is how vision inspires and motivates us.

Holding that image in our mind's eye stimulates and feeds our natural desire. It's like blowing gently on a single flame in a campfire, adding the oxygen that leads to greater combustion. The truth is, each of us contains a tremendous amount of potential energy in the force of our will. We call it will*power*. Vision ignites that energy. When we work towards a vision, we feel alive, engaged and happy.

Vision can be personal as well as organizational. Individual artists, students, entrepreneurs, professionals such as doctors and lawyers – all can be inspired and motivated to succeed by a vision of who they want to become or what they want to accomplish. This might be as straightforward as a painter imaging what their canvas will look like when complete, or an inventor conceptualizing a new design for a technology that does not yet exist.

Getting clear about your creative or professional vision channels and unleashes your energy towards creating it. It's like a mental grappling hook. Imagine you are Batman – or some other flightless superhero. You face a high smooth wall that's impossible to climb. You throw your hook up over the wall, it hooks itself to the top, and then you climb up the attached line. Vision does that for each of us: it helps you reach seemingly unattainable goals, one step at a time.

Some people use a *visual of their vision* to motivate them. If your vision is to help educate children in Africa, then a photograph of African children reading at their desks would be a visual reminder you could place on your wall or as your computer wallpaper. Another motivational tool is to share your vision with others. The act of speaking about your vision fires your imagination, and when the person you are speaking to responds with enthusiasm and interest, it can further fuel your own passion. Social media is another great way to share your vision. By putting the story of what you are seeking to accomplish out into the world, you place some pressure on yourself to actually do it.

Two ambitious sisters we know, Cidalia and Natalia, are great examples of this. They decided they wanted to climb Mt Kilimanjaro together. Both women are professional business leaders in their forties and have never done anything like this before. They decided not just to do the trek for the sake of the adventure, but to also turn it into a fundraiser for DC Children's Hospital. So they set up social media sites and sent emails to all their friends, and raised over $250,000. Their vision grew into something with great purpose and momentum, but putting it out into the world also made it impossible for them to turn back. (We are happy to add the sisters made it to the summit and down again safely).

Vision Statements

If you go to any corporation or organization's website, you are likely to run across a vision statement. Everybody knows it's important to have one. Yet there seems to be great lack of clarity about what a vision statement is, who it is for, why it's important. Vision gets confused with mission, and both are sometimes confused with strategy. Sometimes what is written on the corporate website makes no sense at all, and you can tell the organization has only displayed a "vision statement" because somebody told them they needed one.

Vision, mission and strategy can be well explained by visualizing a simple graphic created by Simon Sinek, the author of *Start with Why*.[10] Sinek's idea is that successful businesses and organizations know their purpose, their "why." But he says when most companies *communicate* with their customers and clients, they start by explaining *what* they do ("We build great computers. Want to buy one?"). A few companies might explain *how* they do what they do ("We combine innovation in design with excellence in customer service"). Not very motivating, Sinek concludes. Why would you buy from this company and not from any other?

When you start with your *why* – explaining the purpose and the values that drive you – you will draw customers to you who see their personal values aligned with yours. Continuing the example of computer companies, Sinek says that Apple's marketing starts with *why*. He paraphrases Apple's vision like this: "In everything we do, we believe in challenging the status quo." Then he moves to the *how:* "We do this by building cutting-edge technology that is sleek, intuitive and easy to use," and finally he gets to the *what:* "We just happen to build great computers. Want to buy one?" The result, according to Sinek, is that Apple has loyal customers who see Apple's values as being similar to their own, and so people will buy a computer or an

MP3 player or a phone from Apple without hesitation. "People don't buy what you make, they buy what you believe," he concludes. (For the record, we would like to note that on its website in early 2015, Apple does not have a clear official vision statement.)

Sinek uses a "Golden Circle" to explain his idea of communicating vision. The golden circle consists of three concentric rings, with the *Why* on the inside, then the *How* in the middle, and finally the *What* on the outer rim. Smart companies communicate from the inside out – starting with *why*. These three rings correspond directly to our topic:

> The *Why* is the Vision Statement
> The *How* is the Mission Statement
> The *What* is the Strategy

Now we can illustrate vision, mission and strategy with the example of an organization we know well, the global environment group WWF. Their vision, articulated on their international office's website is:

> *...to build a future where people live in harmony with nature.*

This phrase matches well the three characteristics we identified of a good vision: a picture of a future that people desire and that will take collective effort to create. It's not a particularly strong visual image, but it's catchy.

Next, WWF's mission statement explains *how* they are going to achieve their vision of this future world:

> *Our mission is to conserve the world's biological diversity, ensuring that the use of renewable natural resources is sustainable.*

And their strategy then explains the specific plan of action they are following to fulfill their mission and attain their vision:

1. *Conserving the Earth's most outstanding places.*
2. *Conserving species that are particularly important for habitat or for people.*

This strategy is then articulated through the list of specific places and species they seek to conserve, and for each, the specific goals they will work towards achieving. In this way, everything the organization does fits into the overall vision they are seeking to create.

Who is your organization's vision statement for? Many people mistakenly think a vision statement is primarily for outsiders and supporters, so that they can get a sense of what the organization is all about. It is true that a clear vision statement does this, and indeed, it's a great tool for finding and creating allies, advocates or customers who want to align themselves with your organization. But this is not the most important role of a vision statement.

First and foremost, a vision statement is for the leaders and staff within the organization. Vision provides them with a sense of direction and purpose. That sense of purpose is what guides everything an organization does and says. Carter Roberts, head of WWF US, once told us that when an organization is created, its founders stamp it with a specific DNA, and that DNA runs through the organization even generations later. Following this metaphor, one could say an organization's vision is the genetic code of its DNA that governs how it expresses itself in the world.

Without a clear vision, an organization's energies can become dissipated as it tries to do too much, works in too many directions, or simply loses its sense of purpose. A clear vision statement helps to keep an organization focused and coherent. In addition – and this is really crucial for any organization – a strong vision makes it possible for strategy and even the mission to be re-evaluated from time to time to make sure they are still aligned.

To sum up, getting your vision statement right is invaluable for an organization *externally* – in terms of how others perceive and interact with you – and *internally* – in terms of how you expend resources, preserve your integrity, adapt to change and look to the future.

Crafting Your Vision Statement

In crafting a vision statement, keep our definition of a strong vision in mind (*a picture of the future that people desire, requiring collective effort*). Add to that the "Four Cs" that make for a good meme (Concise, Concrete, Connected and Catchy). The problem with many vision statements is they get long-winded and bogged down in details. This makes them less memorable and less clear. You want a vision that anyone can hear once and remember.

Exercise

Here's a list of vision statements from a variety of organizations. As you go through, answer these questions:

- Which vision statements seem strongest to you?
- Which of the "Four Cs" of a good meme does each include?
- Overall, does each vision statement leave you with a clear idea about the organization and its corporate DNA?

BBC: To be the most creative organisation in the world.
Human Rights Campaign: Equality for everyone
Oxfam: A just world without poverty

Center for Global Development (development think-tank): Ideas to Action: Independent research for global prosperity

Ducks Unlimited: Filling the skies with waterfowl today, tomorrow and forever.

Habitat for Humanity: A world where everyone has a decent place to live.

The Nature Conservancy: Our vision is to leave a sustainable world for future generations.

WWF: Our vision is to build a future where people live in harmony with nature.

Greenpeace: Solutions to deforestation exist. We're campaigning for zero deforestation globally by 2020.

World Vision: For every child, life in all its fullness; Our prayer for every heart, the will to make it so.

ASPCA: That the United States is a humane community in which all animals are treated with respect and kindness.

Goodwill: Every person has the opportunity to achieve his/her fullest potential and participate in and contribute to all aspects of life.

Save the Children: Our vision is a world in which every child attains the right to survival, protection, development and participation.

Charity: Water believes that we can end the water crisis in our lifetime by ensuring that every person on the planet has access to life's most basic need – clean drinking water.

Clinton Foundation: To implement sustainable programs that improve access worldwide to investment, opportunity, and lifesaving services now and for future generations.

Special Olympics: To transform communities by inspiring people throughout the world to open their minds, accept and include people with intellectual disabilities and thereby anyone who is perceived as different.

Amnesty International: Amnesty International's vision is of a world in which every person enjoys all of the human rights enshrined in the Universal Declaration of Human Rights and other international human rights instruments.

The World Bank Group: Working for a World Free of Poverty

Asian Development Bank: an Asia and Pacific region free of poverty.

African Development Bank: Building today – a better Africa tomorrow.

Inter-American Development Bank: Consolidate a working area of excellence that will position the IDB as a relevant partner in the region and in the international community as a whole in transparency, accountability and anti-corruption policies.

Islamic Development Bank: Our Vision is to be a world-class development bank inspired by Islamic principles.

European Bank for Reconstruction and Development (the website has a "commitment" not a vision statement): The EBRD is committed to furthering progress towards market-oriented economies and the promotion of private and entrepreneurial initiative.

United Nations Development Programme: UNDP's vision is what the organization aspires to be: the UN's lead development agency, and a trusted source of support for countries seeking to solve national and global development challenges. UNDP's vision is based on the fundamental principles of development and human rights enshrined in the UN Charter.

Having gone through this list, we can leave you with a few other principles to keep in mind when designing or revising your vision statement:

- A positive vision of what you want is stronger than a negative vision of what you don't want: "clean drinking water for every person on the planet" is better than "fighting poverty." The second phrase puts more emphasis on the persistence of poverty, but doesn't provide a vision for a positive alternative.

- Don't make it about your organization; make it about creating a better world: "To create a world where people live in harmony with nature" is better than "Aspires to be the UN's lead development agency."
- Be specific about what you want to accomplish, not generic: "A world where everyone has a decent place to live" is better than "To implement sustainable programs that improve access worldwide…"

As a final thought, note that when a group of people discover they have a common vision, they can become a force to reckon with. We develop this further in the final chapter, which is about creating alignment.

Chapter 16

Motivation: The DUH Triangle

It's one thing to share an inspirational vision or idea, another to get people to act on it. Much has been written on the psychology of motivation, some of it wise, much of it dubious. We have boiled it down into three simple principles to keep in mind when you are communicating with specific audiences. We call these principles the *DUH Triangle*. "DUH" stands for Dissatisfaction, Urgency and Hope. Finding the right balance among these three elements is the key to motivating people to act.

Dissatisfaction

Even if you have a great positive vision that inspires you to move forward, that is no guarantee others will want to join you. If people are more or less content with the way things are, it's hard to get them interested in creating change. Or if they think that you've got the issue handled, they don't feel the need to get involved. Dissatisfaction prompts action. If you can rouse people to feel fear or anger, impending loss or outrage, their negative emotions create an urge to change the current situation. That's what makes an indifferent audience ready to move from inertia into action: to fight against tyranny, end hunger, stop child trafficking.

Creating dissatisfaction requires communicating clear facts about current conditions that the audience can accept – even if they don't like what they're hearing. These facts should come from sources they trust, not from those that can too readily be dismissed as politically motivated. Once you paint the current situation clearly and accurately – highlighting the points of dissatisfaction – you can then ask your audience to imagine what the future will look like as these conditions intensify. Put them in the picture of this uncomfortable reality.

Dissatisfaction alone is seldom enough to actually get people to move into action. To create the impulse to act, you need the second element:

Urgency

"So you have a good cause. Why should I do something about it now? I'm busy today. Maybe later." *Later* is our default mode. We procrastinate and in the end nothing changes. It's like going to the dentist. We all know we should get our teeth checked twice a year, but how many of us put it off, until suddenly we get a throbbing ache in the jaw? When an ache turns into pain so acute if feels like an icepick digging into our gums, *then* we're ready to jump into the dentist's chair!

Urgency may be negative, like a toothache, but it can also be a potential gain that will disappear if it's not acted on. At the crassest level, advertisers do this whenever they make a "limited-time offer." Communicate urgency so your audience will want to act *now* – instead of never.

To convey urgency, you have to give people a clear timeline of unfolding events. It's not enough to say, "If we don't act now, all will be lost!" The more precise you are, the better. This is a problem that has bedeviled advocates of acting on Climate Change. Scientists predict a range of possible disastrous points of no return. They are all bound to happen, but because no one can say *exactly* when they will happen, people don't feel the urgency of acting now.

If your own issue has no clear deadline, provide a specific window of opportunity when action can make a difference. For example, those who sell college savings plans are quite persuasive about the value of starting to save for college *now* while your children are young, because the longer you wait, the bigger the annual financial burden of college becomes.

Beyond dissatisfaction and urgency, one final element is essential to motivate action.

Hope

Can you demonstrate that the change in behavior you are calling for will work? Or are you asking your audience to invest in a potential lost cause? We all make mental and emotional calculations that prevent us from wasting our energy. These days, there's a pervasive atmosphere that for the most part, things are getting worse. Political standoffs, debt, inequality, rising crime, impending environmental disaster – this despondent atmosphere makes it easy for people to lapse back into inertia and just accept that things will never get any better. Psychologically, apathy is less stressful than desiring something with all your might that you think probably won't happen.

To inspire realistic hope, the best approach is not only to have a clear vision and the right facts on your side, but also to be able to give compelling real-life examples and stories that show success is possible. For example, if you were trying to have a state government change a biased law, then speaking about how another state made this change as a result of community demand would be a good way to give people hope. If this is the first time such a law has been challenged, then reminding people of different harmful laws overthrown by community action could also work. The main point is, a clear narrative and compelling stories are great ways to convince people that change is possible.

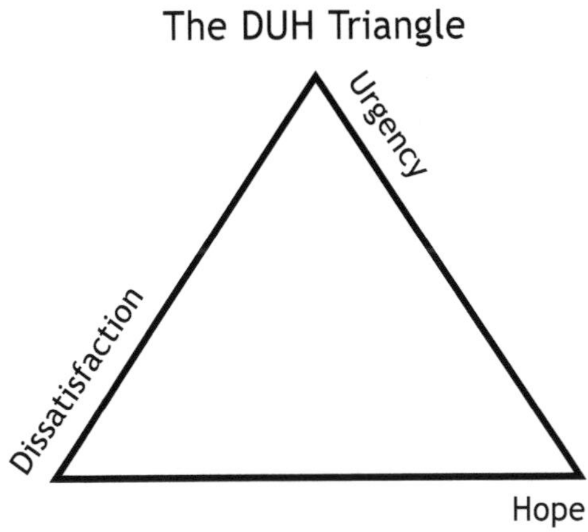

The Dynamic DUH Triangle

The DUH triangle is *dynamic*. This means the three corners shift in importance in response to each specific audience. The better you know your audience, the better you can shift the dimensions of the triangle to emphasize the most effective way to move them into action. For example, some audiences might be very well informed on the discouraging facts of your issue. They don't need you to make them feel more dissatisfied. Perhaps they feel *so* bad they are discouraged. Instead you need to emphasize examples of realistic hope.

Another target audience may have so much hope they think the change you are seeking to accomplish will happen anyway, without their involvement. So they have no sense of urgency. For them you have to stress both the timeline and the need to act *now*. What about potential donors for your work, who are realistically hopeful about your cause and understand the urgency of it, but given the many causes in the world, they don't feel a strong motivation to give to *your* group? In other words, they don't feel enough dissatisfaction. For them you would have to stress why – from their point of view – this particular issue needs their action and support.

Tim saw an example of the DUH triangle at work some years ago when he was on a writing assignment in Thailand. He was writing a story on the Global Environment Facility's small grants program. He visited a coastal village that had received a grant to replant and restore a tropical mangrove forest on the community's common land. The story sounded very straight-forward. But actually, Tim found out the villagers didn't want the grant at first.

The village leaders said that when the GEF approached them about a grant, people were apathetic to the idea. Although their forest was quite run down – many trees cut, trash on the forest floor, declining quantity of medicinal leaves and other forest products to harvest – nobody was ready to do anything about it. So in terms of the elements of the DUH triangle, at this point they were dissatisfied with the status quo, they knew there was practical hope to improve the situation because of this grant…but there was no urgency that impelled them to action. Then one day, a villager spotted a couple of strangers in the forest with surveying equipment. They knew these were Thai government surveyors, and they knew what that meant. Under Thai law, if a community allows its forest areas to degrade beyond a certain point, the central government can permanently confiscate the land and turn it into a protected area that is out of bounds for the community!

The villager raced back to the community elders with the news. It jolted them. They immediately applied for and received the grant. Following its terms, the whole community went into the swamps to clean up the trash and replant the mangroves. They showed Tim photographs of the mayor and police chief smiling broadly as they sloshed around in the muck by the water's edge. After the initial campaign, they mutually enforced a ban on foraging as the forest regrew. Only when dissatisfaction, urgency and hope all came together did the community act.

The villagers told Tim their story with much pride. A woman elder told him their medicinal plants were flourishing again, and they had resumed limited harvesting. She recalled that the leaders from a neighboring village had even come to beg permission to forage in the newly revitalized land – because this other community had let their own forest degrade. With a chiding tone in her voice, the elder said, "But I told them, 'No! You can't use our forest! You must learn to take care of your own resources, the way we do it!'"

Keeping the DUH triangle in your head reminds you that you are never just speaking to a generic audience. When you seek to motivate, you are connecting with real people, with their own complex desires, knowledge and maps of what the world is like and what's important. Ultimately, the DUH triangle awakens people to their own sense of agency: that they have the power to create change in their world.

Chapter 17

Transformational Storytelling

Once upon a time nobody told stories in business meetings, at conferences or during media interviews. People focused on the facts. Data, statistics, the bottom line – information mattered most. Then management gurus like Steven Denning came along and told everyone that storytelling was the "Secret Language of Leadership" (the title of one of his best-selling books on the subject). Gradually more and more people became convinced that you had to tell stories in the workplace. Soon everyone was telling stories. Everyone was expecting stories. Everyone was talking about the transformational power of stories. But there was still a problem – the actual evidence for this transformational power was not so obvious. Everyone believed in stories, but in the back of their minds, they were recalling the tale of the Emperor's New Clothes…

So what's the problem with storytelling? The answer is simple: in a professional context, people usually tell *boring* stories. The good news is that in our experience running storytelling workshops, it's relatively easy to teach people to tell riveting and transformational stories. It typically takes us about 3 hours to take the dullest bureaucrat you can imagine, and make them capable of enrapturing an audience.

In this chapter, we will take you through the five elements of great storytelling. First, we'd like to explain why well-told stories can be transformational.

Stories open our minds and our hearts. When someone tells a good story, our minds shift gears. We relax and enjoy the experience in a different way than when a speaker is relaying purely factual information. Neuroeconomics researcher Dr Paul Zak[11] and his team at Claremont University have discovered that certain kinds of stories affect the brain's production of mood-altering chemicals. For example, character-driven stories produce oxytocin, a neurochemical that makes us feel trust and safety. In other words, stories put us into a receptive state of rapport. In our storytelling workshops, we can sense the energy in the room shift dramatically as people start to tell their stories to one another. The participants almost instantly become open, relaxed and energized in a magical, positive way.

Stories focus our attention better than a presentation of facts alone. According to Dr Zak's research, the elements of tension and anticipation in a well-told story trigger the release of cortisol, the chemical that makes us focus and remember things clearly. Information encoded in a story can thus be recalled much more easily than a collection of informational facts, and we'll remember it far longer.

Stories are convincing because they portray information in the context of human experience. We process facts and data in the left hemisphere of our brains, which allows us to evaluate the information at arm's length. But a good narrative draws us into our imagination. We put ourselves in the shoes of the characters, and experience the action almost as if it's happening to us. Since we tend to trust our *own* experience, information delivered in a story feels more convincing.

Stories make us care. The oxytocin triggered by character-driven stories also makes us feel connection and empathy. When we put ourselves in the shoes of the characters in the story, they start to matter to us. This shift in perspective can actually help people step out of a mindset that has become inflexible or intolerant. In this way storytelling can be a powerful technique for helping someone reframe his or her thinking.

Stories make us believe change is possible. When we hear a story of one person overcoming injustice in an oppressive society, we learn that victory can be won. If change can be accomplished once, then it can be accomplished again. Stories enable us to imagine how our own actions can create change in a similar way. This lays the groundwork for transformation.

Stories motivate us to act. By setting up a new pattern or paradigm of what is possible, stories rouse our passions and motivate us. For example, if we hear a story of courage, our own sense of courage may be awakened. The chemical oxytocin also triggers us for cooperation, and so storytelling is a perfect vehicle for inspiring a team to unite and work together towards a common purpose.

What does it take to learn to tell a great story that produces these benefits? In our storytelling workshop, we break it down to five key elements.

1. A Good Beginning: The Red Chair

It's painful to have to force yourself to listen to a story when it limps along after a slow beginning. It's almost impossible to grab your audience and make an impact once you've lost them. A great teaching example of how to start a story can be found on the BBC's *The Graham Norton Show*. At the end of each show the host invites members of the audience to come up and sit in a giant red chair and tell the best story of their lives. The catch is, if the stories bore Norton, he pulls a silver lever and the chair flips over backwards, sending the storyteller flying with their feet scrabbling in the air – to the great amusement of the audience. Most contestants are flipped almost immediately, because they start their stories with dull preambles like this:

"I spent a summer teaching windsurfing in Turkey—" (Flip!)

"I was in Israel on a vacation, and I got on a bus for 4 hours—" (Flip!)

Our favorite Red Chair story was told by a very respectable-looking woman in her sixties who began like this: "I used to ride an Arab stallion in the desert..." After this first line, Norton burst in, exclaiming *"Hello!* If the story continues this way, we're loving it!"

The key is to begin your story in the *middle* of the action, not before the action. Instead of starting by explaining the details that set the story up, bring your audience into the scene with a moment of danger, suspense or wonder. Here are a few great examples of this from people in our workshops:

"I didn't understand a word of the Cambodian language, but I instantly understood the meaning of what our guide had just screamed: we had wandered into a minefield..."

"I'd like to tell you about the day I realized sometimes planes *do* fall out of the sky..."

"I looked at the orangutan, and the orangutan looked at me. I could tell he was thinking, 'I can take her...'"

"I want to tell you about the day I died...and the only reason I'm here to tell the tale is because a curious nurse lifted up the sheet over my face. She'd never seen a dead body before..."

2. Vivid Details Capture the Imagination

The magic of a story is that with just our words we can create a movie in our listeners' minds. This transports our audience to another world. The "special effects" that make this happen are vivid sensory descriptions that shift the listener from the analytic left side of their brain into the right hemisphere, where images and sense data are processed. It doesn't take a lot of description, just a few vivid details. Here are two examples from our workshop participants:

"In a Sumatran rainforest, all you see is shades of dark green. Something white in the distance stands out like a beacon. It can only mean one thing: bone – in this case, the skull of a rhinoceros, killed by poachers…"

"I looked over the wall of our house in Bombay, and on the other side, in a dusty construction site, I saw one of the women workers. She was tying the foot of her baby with a cord to a rock, tethering him, so that as she worked carrying piles of rubble in her basket, her child would not crawl away…"

To make your stories vivid, think about the experience you are going to share and imagine yourself back in the moment, reliving it. As the sense impressions come to you, write them all down. Then select those that most powerfully evoke the key details of the scene. Be sure to include more than just sight and sound. Impressions of smell, taste, touch, as well as bodily sensations and emotions all create an impression of vividness that brings a story to life.

3. Drama Creates Tension and Suspense

Most stories told at conferences or in presentations are boring because they are predictable. For example, in international development circles stories typically go like this: "A community is poor. Our agency comes along, analyzes the problem and builds a project. Now the community is happy." Sure, there is action. But the events are totally uninteresting. It's the obstacles, struggles, risks and unique challenges to overcome that bring a story to life.

To make a story interesting, focus on what went wrong. What crises occurred? How did the people in the story overcome them? This creates tension and anticipation. Then cortisol, the stress hormone, is released into our brains. We feel the danger, the urgency. It focuses our minds. It makes us wonder what's going to happen next. Anticipation puts us in a heightened state of awareness in which we remember things more clearly than in our normal floating-along-through-life state of awareness. One way to get your audience into that state is by telling a harrowing story that sheds light on the larger issue you are talking about. We've heard surprising tales from bureaucrats and managers of being stuck in a war zone with bombs exploding around them, or being gored by an elephant, or being robbed at knifepoint.

Of course, workplace stories can't all involve being chased by elephants. One of the best stories we've heard in one of our workshops was from a Korean man, a development bank country director, who told us a story that forever changed the way he looked at water. His development bank had completed and closed a hydropower dam project in Laos when an NGO representative showed up at his office with complaints about communities downstream suffering water shortage problems. Since the project was closed, he could have told her, "Sorry, nothing we can do!" But she spoke passionately about how villagers downstream found their crops had withered and their fish disappeared. They were planning to protest and blockade roads. The director realized this would damage his bank's credibility. More importantly, if people were suffering as a result of this dam, then he and his bank had a moral obligation to put things right. So he agreed to reopen the project and conduct an investigation – a terribly risky move. He himself went down to the area and discovered there were legitimate grievances, which his organization worked to fix. He admitted this was not a successful project, but it was the one that taught him the most in his long career.

4. Character

We enter into a story through the characters. This makes us care about what happens, and makes us care about them. We put ourselves in their shoes and feel the emotions they experience. Stories give us empathy, and can inspire us to act. The problem we often encounter with workplace stories is that the characters seem fake – a client or a customer – but not a real person. A story that starts with: "Mohammed is a poor farmer in Bangladesh…" but gives no specifics makes the person seem like a generic "project beneficiary." People can't connect to a cardboard cutout.

Resist this tendency to make up characters or create a "composite" character. Tell stories about real people. Your audience will sense the difference. If you are a manager conducting site visits and you meet people involved in your work, be sure to ask their names. If they have an interesting story to tell, write it down. When you introduce these real people in your story, provide at least one vivid detail about them. One of our participants told a story about a Mongolian project partner who "had a real glint in his eye." Another participant who worked on tiger conservation told us about a Nepalese farmer who had become a strong advocate for protecting tigers – though he had a large scar from a tiger attack across the right side of his face.

We learn about characters through their actions in the story. What people do, especially in the midst of crisis or hardship, tells us a lot about who they are, and this is what makes us care, connect and enter into the story. Ngozi Okonjo-Iweala, the finance minister of Nigeria, tells a riveting story in a TED Talk of how as a teenage girl she carried her sick baby sister through a war zone to save her life. The girl was dying of malaria, and young Ngozi had to strap her on her back and walk 10 kilometers in the burning heat to find help. When she arrived at a church where a doctor had set up a clinic, there were a thousand people trying to get in through the door. With her sick sister on her back, she crawled through the legs of the crowd to the side of the church and climbed in through a window. The doctor told her she was just in the nick of time; her sister wouldn't have survived much longer. The doctor gave the child a shot of chloroquine, and saved her life. We learn so much about Okonjo-Iweala's character from her actions – her determination and resourcefulness in overcoming obstacles.

Character is especially important in development stories, because the generic examples of project beneficiaries often portray people living in poverty as victims who depend on others for their rescue and survival. While sometimes this is true – people do need to be rescued in the midst of disasters – when you make a "poor person" into a victim, you deny him or her agency.

We heard a great story of a character with agency, a woman who broke a gender barrier in her hometown in Kerala, India. She was an unskilled laborer who worked at a construction site. She qualified for a skills-training program and selected plumbing as her trade. No other woman had *ever* become a plumber before in her town. However, after completing her training, no construction company would hire her. They didn't trust that a woman could do the job well. She was no better off than before.

Instead of giving up, she started doing kitchen repairs for her housewife neighbors. Then she started getting referrals by word of mouth. Apparently, male plumbers used to leave a mess when fixing the plumbing. However, she would always leave the kitchens and bathrooms spotlessly clean. Soon this woman had built a successful local business and was taking on young women like herself as apprentices.

When your characters have agency, your audience can be inspired by their actions to see how change is possible.

Finally, when you yourself are a character in your story, it can create a sense of authenticity, trust and shared conviction. We worked with Crawford Allan, a leader in the global fight against wildlife crime. In his talks, he tells the story of the moment that changed his life. He was working as a detective in London and his team was following a lead on a smuggling case. Crawford recalled entering a room filled with the carcasses of hundreds of stuffed, endangered species. "A dead zoo," he called it. He spoke about holding the severed and preserved head of a chimpanzee in his hand. The wrongness of it filled him with such conviction that he vowed to do whatever it took to end this kind of brutality. Everyone in the room felt his passion and conviction, and it made us all want to support him in his mission.

5. Resolution

When the resolution to a good story is satisfying, our brains get a hit of the pleasure chemical, dopamine. But the end must also be surprising in some way. Think for example of the twist at the end of the movie *Planet of the Apes*. The main character has fought his way to freedom – but in the last frame he discovers his ordeal has been on planet Earth in the distant future. Though he survived, human civilization had perished.

Fortunately, your stories don't need quite such earth-shattering endings. You can use one simple tactic to help you find your way to the unexpected. Focus on what has changed as a result of the story. For example, the Korean country manager ended his story about fixing the Laos dam's harmful impacts by concluding, "This experience made me think about water differently. It made me realize water is about energy, food and environment all together. You can't think about only one side of its impact. You have to see the full picture."

By concluding with an element of change, you can highlight the transformation in your story. For example, Ngozi Okonjo-Iweala ended her story about saving her sister from dying of malaria by saying, "My sister grew up to become a doctor herself, and now she is saving other lives."

Transformational Storytelling

Transformational stories show us that change is possible. They show us how human agency can make the world a better place. Ngozi Okonjo-Iweala's sister, the Korean country manager and the woman plumber in Kerala are all examples of this kind of positive change. When we learn about transformation through a well-told story, it feels almost as if the story happened to us, and we integrate it into our understanding of the world as personal, rather than abstract, knowledge.

If change can be accomplished once, then it can be accomplished again. In this way the logic of transformational stories convinces us that change is possible. Stories with this transformational dimension can be a powerful tool for helping people reframe how they see the world. Often people aren't motivated because they believe change is not possible. Stories can shift them out of their old beliefs and into something new. That shift helps move them to act.

Narrative and Mythos

We conclude with a final and very important element of storytelling: how narrative shapes our understanding of the world. Each of us makes sense of the world through stories that tell about how things are. We use the word *myth* – from the Greek *mythos* – to describe ancient stories of gods and heroes. But in this broader sense, *mythos* means any story people believe that helps them understand their origins, values, and sense of purpose or destiny.

When you speak to your audiences' sense of mythos you can move them deeply, and motivate them to care and to act. Think for example of Abraham Lincoln's famous Gettysburg Address, in which he speaks of the founding of the United States on the premise of freedom for all, the bloodshed in the civil war as a struggle to preserve that freedom, and the task of the nation in the aftermath of the war to rebuild so that "government of the people, for the people, by the people shall not perish from the earth." In evoking mythos, he set out to inspire all citizens for the difficult task ahead.

This is where storytelling intersects with vision. When you tell an audience *their* story, a story in which the ending has yet to be written, a story in which they are the actors who have the agency to influence their own fate, then you have become a transformational communicator.

To sum up, the key elements of a great story are:

- A good beginning
- Vividness
- Drama
- Character
- A resolution that satisfies and surprises the audience

When you put these together, you become a transformational storyteller, and a master communicator.
We would like to end with a riveting and elegantly concise story we recently heard from a Chinese woman economist:

"I'd like to tell you a story about the day my father beat me up. I was 19, and my parents had found and read my diary. They discovered their suspicions were true – I had participated in the Tiananmen Square demonstrations. That evening my father came to me in tears. He shocked me by telling me I had once had a brother. He died when he was a baby, before I was born. This was during the Cultural Revolution, when my parents were politically active and were persecuted. My father told me he vowed he would never lose another child to political activism…I tell this story to explain why for so many Chinese, stability is the most important social value."

Chapter 18

Alignment: Expanding Your Influence

To change the world, even just one corner of it, you can't do it alone. You need a strong, collaborative network. Often, however, when we attempt to work with others to achieve a common goal, we end up in power struggles, negotiations and entanglements that can sap our energy and leave us frustrated and falling far short of our ambitions.

Alignment, as we define it, offers a different path. Instead of finding a common goal to rally around, alignment depends on finding a common purpose. A goal is an external objective. A purpose is internal; it's about values and vision. Finding a common purpose transcends specific objectives and creates a bond that makes you feel part of the same tribe or team as your collaborators.

The TV show *Survivor* is a great example of what happens when people only have a common goal. Season after season we watch alliances form with the mutual goal of making it to the "final five" or the "final three" on the show. Yet because the ultimate goal is for an individual to win over all others, these alliances almost always break down. Somebody wants to get the jump on the rest and betrays the group.

A common goal is a means. A common purpose is an end.

Contrast the *Survivor* type of alliance with one of the most famous cases of alignment the world has ever known: the Battle of Thermopylae, which was not long ago made into a Hollywood film, *300*. This historic event is considered one of the greatest displays of courage in the face of overwhelming odds – and its outcome decisively altered the course of history.

In 480 BC the Persian emperor Xerxes invaded Greece, determined to add it to his vast empire. A massive army, estimated at 100,000 men, marched on Athens and central Greece from the north. But to reach their goal, the Persians were forced to travel through a narrow pass at Thermopylae. For 2 solid days, a band of 300 Spartan warriors blocked the pass, holding at bay the entire Persian attack force. Ultimately, the Persians defeated the 300, but the fortitude of the Spartans who died at Thermopylae inspired the Greeks. Although they lost the battle and Athens fell, the Greeks refused to surrender. Later that year they won two stunning victories. Xerxes retreated, and most of the defeated Persian forces died of disease and starvation as they fled from Greece.

Had the Greeks lost heart, there would have been no golden age of Athenian democracy with all it has given to the world – elected leaders, the birth of reason, dramatic theater, trial by jury, free speech and universal public education of citizens.

To the 300 Spartans, their aligned vision of a free Greece was worth dying for. We might say alignment creates a common purpose worth living for.

When we teach alignment to our clients, we do it at the end of a 6-day Master Communicators program. This is because to effectively create alignment you need to know just about every other skill in this book, including messaging, authority, rapport, cueing, framing, vision and storytelling. Here are a few additional techniques you can easily use to increase your ability to align yourself with others:

Find the Right People

Your existing network is your best resource. However, people often don't see their network. It's a sort of hazy web hanging in space. To concretize this web, take a large sheet of paper and draw a small circle in the center with your name in it. If there is a particular purpose you are working towards, like moving a project, program or piece of legislation forward, write that at the top of the page. Now you can map your network: draw lines connecting you to others in your work or personal life. Next, take a colored pencil or marker and use that color to connect you with those on the alignment map who could help you achieve your goal in any way. It could be that some names on your map are bridges to other networks of influence.

The result will probably look like the sort of diagram you see in detective shows on TV – with a murder victim connected to dozens of potential suspects and witnesses. It doesn't matter if your diagram looks messy or chaotic; creating the display so you can visualize it is what counts.

If you are focusing within your company, get hold of an organizational chart. Circle your name, and then connect it with others with whom you have a connection within the organization. You can use different colors and thicknesses of lines to indicate the strength of the connection, whether it is personal or professional, etc.

Here are two lessons some of our participants learned through this exercise:

One thought leader we worked with was attempting to influence several governments across South America to forge an economic policy agreement. She needed to align with others with a similar vision: individuals who would be willing to use their influence to get the key decision-makers to sign off on it. By simply diagramming her relationships she quickly realized there were three people she knew in Washington DC who could help her – and in fact, she knew one of them would be meeting with a visiting South American president the following week. But it had never occurred to her to think of asking for his support on this issue.

Another example was a woman we worked with who was in charge of strategic communications within her organization. She wanted to map the relationships between her unit and the rest of the organization. She was astonished at the result. It revealed that her team had very strong relationships with two thirds of the organization, but very few lines connecting them with the final third – and she had always wondered why this department was so unresponsive to her strategic initiatives!

Here's a simplified example of one of these maps:

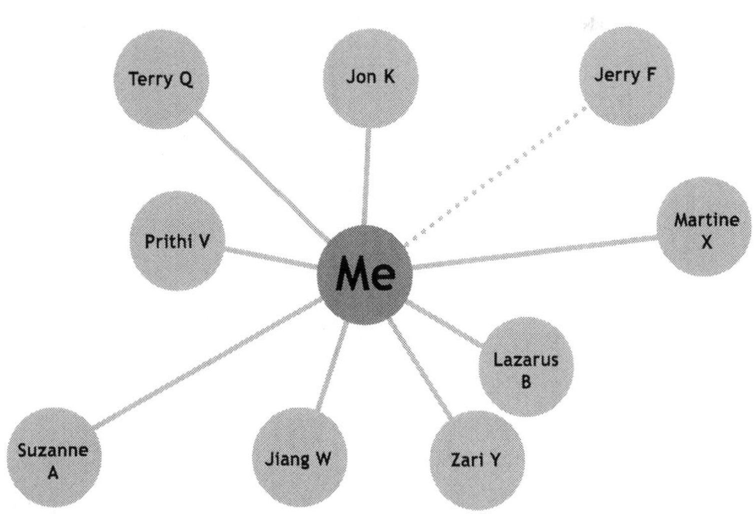

There's an additional level you can add to this if you are looking to connect with specific influencers. It's similar to the concept of "Six Degrees of Separation." This is the theory that we are potentially connected to everyone else on the planet by links of no more than six people. The "Kevin Bacon Game" best illustrates this principle. How many people would it take to connect you to Kevin Bacon? You probably know someone who knows someone who knows someone famous in Hollywood, and that person would know Kevin Bacon. That would be four degrees of separation between you and Kevin Bacon. Diagramming your relationships can help you find the best route to connecting with key people you might want to create an alignment with.

Connect around Shared Values and Vision

Here's where rapport, vision, framing and storytelling all come into play, especially if you are reaching out to people you don't already know. When we find someone with a common vision and values, there's this tremendous burst of energy, like an atomic fusion reaction. It is as if we intuitively sense not only the great potential of aligning ourselves with others, but also that this use of our energy will bring us some kind of joy. You "click" with them, and that sense of "clicking" is the sound of connection. When people find a sense of common purpose, they will work long and hard together, often without any thought to financial reward.

If you are meeting someone in order to gauge the potential for alignment, it is important to listen to the stories they tell, the heroes they describe and the metaphors they use. These reveal what philosopher of psychology Shai Tubali calls the *primal narrative*. These are the stories we tell ourselves about how life is, and about finding our place in the world.[12]

For example, someone who uses sports metaphors and tells

stories about big wins or losses in life might have a primal narrative centered on competition. If you have a similar affinity for competition, this might spur the two of you to want to join the "same team" in some common endeavor. The purpose is to see if you can find a common value. This will allow you to recognize each other as belonging to the same tribe. As soon as this happens, a sense of "in group" identity gets created which becomes the basis for collaboration.

Similarly, if you are seeking to connect with others, think about what you value as ends in themselves. What stories do you tell that reveal your passion and vision? As we were mastering this concept ourselves several years ago, we realized we were not doing as good a job as we could at engaging new clients around the courses we were most excited about. So we changed our tactics. Instead of describing the content of our programs, we led with our passion for creating transformation through communications. This resulted in a remarkable shift. We found ourselves working much more with leaders who shared our passion.

When you "click" with someone around shared values and vision, you find yourselves searching for ways to collaborate. How can you do this most efficiently?

Compromise

Compromise seems negative to many people. It implies a power struggle: giving up something in order to get something. In work and personal relationships we often approach compromise like negotiators seeking to maximize our gain and minimize our loss. But when it comes to alignment, *compromise* means something different. It goes back to the Latin root of the word, which implies a "com" – meaning "together," and "promise" – meaning to "send forward." So compromise can be considered a "sending forward together," which is a great definition of alignment.

Mature compromise is not a power struggle. Instead, you can acknowledge that the other person has a strong and independent will. In fact, you want that other person to be as powerful as possible. You also want them to stay different from you, because that difference brings different skills and resources, and makes you more powerful when aligned. Think for example of the comic-book heroes, *The Avengers.* Iron Man, Thor, Black Widow – each brings their unique power to the team, which is what makes them strong.

Compromise, then, can be a way of working together that allows each of you to maximize your strength. Sometimes this means yielding to each other when there is conflict. Sometimes it means being willing to hold the tension of different views until you can find a way forward.

We often do this ourselves when we create a new course. Tim, with his background as a non-fiction author, relishes complexity. Tim prefers to design course modules that contain a comprehensive theoretical explanation so participants can understand how fascinating these ideas are, and where they come from. As a former radio host and editor, Teresa is attuned to the ease with which a listener will be able to grasp content. To her, shorter is almost always better. Information should be practical, and any theoretical content must be followed by an example of its application. We've learned that when we value each other's perspective *more* than getting our own way, we come up with something better than either of us could have designed on our own.

One of the most amazing organizations we've worked with that puts alignment into practice is an NGO based in Washington named Machik.[13] This is a group that works with Tibetans inside Tibet on education, environmental and social issues across the plateau. Once a year they bring together Chinese policy researchers from Beijing with respected Tibetan community and civic leaders for a unique discussion and exchange on the challenges of governance in Tibet. Previously these two groups never interacted. Most people are aware that these are uncertain times in Tibet. Yet the people who come together for this dialogue have forged a bond and commitment around the vision of a peaceful future for Tibet.

In sum, alignment multiplies your ability to create transformation. The truth is, most people in the world follow their own desires, and often these push and pull us in different directions, so that the overall result is not momentum towards a particular goal, but a global inertia. You could even conceive of society as like a giant hot-air balloon or floating blimp. It's vast, but motionless. However, if you blew on it from one direction with enough people and sustained force, sooner or later the balloon would respond to the pressure and begin to move in the direction you push it.

That's the power alignment can create. It's a force that can change the world.

References

1. Collier, Richard, *The World in Flames*. Harmondsworth: Penguin, 1980, p. 352.
2. Jim Yong Kim, president of the World Bank, paraphrased quote from NPR interview on *Morning Edition*, 7 December 2012.
3. Kelly McGonigal, "How to Make Stress Your Friend." TedGlobal, 2013. https://www.ted.com/talks/kelly_mcgonigal_how_to_make_stress_your_friend.
4. Able, Ernest; Kruger, Michael, "Smile Intensity in Photographs Predicts Longevity," *Psychological Science*, Wayne State University, 4-8-2010.
5. Carney, Dana R.; Cuddy, Amy J. C.; Yap, Andy J., "Power Posing – Brief Nonverbal Displays Affect Neuroendocrine Levels and Risk Tolerance," *Journal of the Association for Psychological Science*, October 2010.
6. Amy Cuddy, "Your Body Language Shapes Who You Are," TedGlobal 2012. http://www.ted.com/talks/amy_cuddy_your_body_language_shapes_who_you_are
7. For more information on how to improve your voice: Dr Susan Miller, *Be Heard the First Time*, Capitol Books, 2006.
8. Dr Dan M. Kahan, *Washington Post* Blog, 23 February 2015. http://www.washingtonpost.com/blogs/monkey-cage/wp/2015/02/23/you-can-change-the-minds-of-climate-change-skeptics-heres-how/
9. Carla Harris, *Expect to Win: 10 Proven Strategies for Thriving in the Workplace*, Plume, 2009.
10. Simon Sinek, *Start with Why: How Great Leaders Inspire Everyone to Take Action*, Portfolio Books, 2011.
11. Dr Paul Zak, "The Neuroscience of Narrative," *Cerebrum*, www.Dana.org, February 2015.
12. Shai Tubali and Tim Ward, *Indestructible You: Building a Self*

that Can't Be Broken, Changemakers Books, 2015.
13. For more information: www.machik.org

About the Authors

Teresa Erickson and Tim Ward are co-owners of Intermedia Communications Training, Inc. Together they have designed and led hundreds of communications workshops around the world, working with organizations such as WWF, the World Bank, International Monetary Fund, the Asian and African Development Banks, the World Health Organization and the United Nations.

Born in Portugal, Teresa worked with the Voice of America for 19 years, from 1980 to 1999, as a producer, editor, and host for 7 years of VOA's flagship public affairs program broadcast worldwide to 90 million listeners a week. Her reporting has won numerous awards and she has voiced award-winning documentaries for broadcast in Brazil and Portugal.

Tim is a former print journalist and a well-known author in his native Canada. He has written eight books, including the best-seller, *What the Buddha Never Taught*, and *Indestructible You* (with Shai Tubali). Tim is also publisher of Changemakers Books.

Contact:
www.intermediacommunicationstraining.com
twitter: @MessageCraft
www.facebook.com/Intermediact

Changemakers publishes books for individuals committed to transforming their lives and transforming the world. Our readers seek to become positive, powerful agents of change. Changemakers books inform, inspire, and provide practical wisdom and skills to empower us to create the next chapter of humanity's future.

Please visit our website at www.changemakers-books.com